God Is in Love with You

God Is in Love
with You

Valerie Love

www.urbanchristianonline.net

Urban Books, LLC
78 East Industry Court
Deer Park, NY 11729

God Is in Love with You Copyright © 2009 Valerie Love

ISBN 13: 978-1-60162-820-6
ISBN 10: 1-60162-820-X

First Mass Market Printing February 2012
First Trade Paperback Printing August 2009
Printed in the United States of America

10 9 8 7 6 5 4 3 2 1

This is a work of fiction. Any references or similarities to actual events, real people, living, or dead, or to real locales are intended to give the novel a sense of reality. Any similarity in other names, characters, places, and incidents is entirely coincidental.

Distributed by Kensington Publishing Corp.
Submit Wholesale Orders to:
Kensington Publishing Corp.
C/O Penguin Group (USA) Inc.
Attention: Order Processing
405 Murray Hill Parkway
East Rutherford, NJ 07073-2316
Phone: 1-800-526-0275
Fax: 1-800-227-9604

This book is dedicated to you, dear reader. It is an offering to every beloved soul who has experienced the pain of loss or the imagined absence of God. May this book serve as a balm that coats and soothes your soul and effects a tremendous healing in your spirit. Hallelujah!

". . . Yes, I have Loved you with an everlasting love; therefore with loving-kindness have I drawn you *and* continued My faithfulness to you." Jeremiah 31:3 (AMP)

"He who most greatly loves most greatly lives." Ernest Holmes *Science of Mind*

Contents

Acknowledgments

Writing this book has been a labor of love. At times, I hated writing it. At other times, I relished it. Through it all, I prayed, breathed, and persisted. I am grateful to the end of my earthly days for God's Holy Spirit, which strengthens and renews me, and serves as a gentle reminder that all things are possible with God.

I am deeply grateful for the spiritual foundation I received from James and Jacqueline McIntosh, my parents. Thank you. You are forever in my heart.

Many thanks to all whose hands, hearts, and minds gently guided and shaped this work, including Audra Barrett, my agent, Joylynn Jossel, the book's editor at Urban Christian, and the entire Urban Christian family. Thank you.

I am pleased and delighted to thank my husband, Ronnie Soloman Ware, Sr., for his steadfast love and affection. I love you, Jelly Biscuit.

My children are an immense joy and add the sweetness necessary to live a well-balanced and full life. Thank you Cory, Sarai, Varonika, and Ronnie Jr.

A hearty thank you goes to my Inner Visions family, including Omayra Castro, for standing with me and holding the vision for this book as I completed it, and Rev. Dr. Iyanla Vanzant, who is a wellspring of inspiration.

My heartfelt gratitude to you all.

Valerie Love

How to Use This Book

You may read this book through in its entirety, or you may choose to throw it open whenever you please. Because we live in an ordered and orderly universe, if you decide to throw the book open anytime you feel so inclined, know that whatever pages the book opens to will be precisely what you need to read in that moment. Try the exercise with intention.

Affirmations appear at the end of each chapter under the heading *Thoughts for Today*. State them emphatically out loud. The Word creates. Your spoken word carries immense creative vibratory power in your world. Use this power wisely by affirming your soul's truth.

When you've finished reading this book, please re-read any portions that resonate with you or any portions which have not fully integrated into the depths of your being. Re-read those portions as many times as is necessary for you to fully believe—with your entire mind, body, and soul—just how deeply God is in love with you.

After you've completed reading and re-reading the words herein, please pass this book along to someone who may be unsure of God's unconditional love. Pray to meet such a person and he or she will appear.

Why I Wrote This Book

That was then, this is now.

I was born and raised in Harlem, USA. The "hood" some would call it, where living with roaches and mice was commonplace, and seeing rats on the streets rummaging through trash was an everyday occurrence. I grew up curiously witnessing people who lived on the streets, or at least were often found there, who couldn't easily solve their problems and so chose to turn to heroin, alcohol, or crack cocaine to do the job for them.

I've never met nor have I ever laid eyes on my biological father. If I walked past him on the street, I'd have no clue. When he found out his nineteen-year-old girlfriend was pregnant, I guess it was too much for him to handle, so he didn't.

When I was young, a relative decided to learn more about sex, and chose me as the learning modality. The terror, shame, and guilt, which can and often does arise in a young person who has been inappropriately sexually affronted, is heavy and requires a mountain of healing.

I've been overweight and out of shape from using food as a panacea.

I've been bedridden with depression such that I could barely raise my head to care for my new-born baby daughter. Thanks to breastfeeding, she was fed every day.

I've been financially bankrupt twice, and I've experienced emotional turmoil as my family's home went into foreclosure three times. I've had tax liens on my home, and voluntarily surrendered a nearly new vehicle, reported to the credit bureaus as a repossession.

I've been divorced, and have spent several years as a single mother. I've been in an abusive relationship as well as an adulterous one.

Obviously, I didn't come from privilege, or fortune, or fame. The silver spoon was far from my mouth.

None of that matters, because that was then and this is now.

Now, I live each day in gratitude and deep love.

I live my soul's purpose with passion and power.

I enjoy my days doing what I love: writing, and teaching how to use spiritual laws and principles to effect radical healing, growth, and personal transformation. I am blessed to do what makes my heart sing. More importantly, I am blessed to be the one who makes my heart sing.

I am free to explore creative ideas and transform them from the invisible realm of thought to the physical realm of fruition, bringing me joy and fulfillment as I live my dream of being an inspiration.

My business endeavors are thriving.

I own homes that are spacious and beautifully appointed, and I currently reside in a loving nest I named Slice of Heaven. Thankfully, the elements that convert a neighborhood into a "hood" are not present in my new community.

I find comfort in relationships that feed and nurture me.

I enjoy heartfelt communion in a spiritual community, which supports me in living in excellence, grace, and balance.

I am blessed to enjoy vibrant and radiant health.

I am caught up in the rapture of God's unconditionally loving embrace.

I am happy.

I am fulfilled.

I am joyful beyond words.

I am intentionally living my dreams.

This brings me to the reason I wrote this book, which is really twofold.

I've noticed, and you may have too, that there are few people who actually seem to be happy, joyful, fulfilled, and aware of a deep, abiding love within. They are the folks we hold in high esteem who dare to create lives of their own design and desire, and who do it with boldness and courage. They reach the highest heights in their chosen arenas, whether in the arts, spirituality, music, or some other endeavor. When I observe folks who inspire me, I silently muse, *what a great example*.

At the other end of the spectrum, there are those among us who are hurting. Some have forgotten love and what it feels like. Some are looking for love in all the wrong places, and, of course, end up not finding it. Some of our brothers and sisters are strung out, like the folks standing on street corners I used to see in my early years. Some turn to alcohol or other painkillers to douse their troubles, albeit briefly. Some are locked up, in society's attempt to figure out what to do with folks we don't fully understand and have yet to discover how to fully serve.

I wrote this book for the latter group—for the folks who are hurting. I know what it's like to hurt, to look for love outside of oneself and not find it. This book is intended to be a healing balm. There is but one solution to all life's hurts: God's unconditional and unfathomable love, which is right now expressing in you, as you, through you, and for you.

Part two of why I wrote this book is because there's much in my heart and in my experiences to share. I pray that sharing my continuing journey of living in love and grace becomes a catalyst that fans a flame in you to do the same.

I am writing this book to share how I've been able to recreate my world in harmonious accord with Love, and how I'm continuing to work the ever-evolving and unfolding process daily.

I am writing to tell the story of how I turned lemons into the sweetest lemonade and how you can too. Anyone can. We each have the God-given power to triumph.

I pray you enjoy this tome and, most importantly, I pray you'll choose to live in Love.

Introduction

God is in love with you. God is head-over-heels, crazy in love with you. You may not believe or know this now, so my prayer for you is that you experience a radical shift into absolutely knowing and feeling God's unconditional love. As mentioned earlier, we live in an orderly and ordered universe, which provides assurance that you will pick up this book and read exactly the parts you need in the moment. Open your heart so that the following words may find a home in you, and elicit transformation.

This book is not written for any particular religion. It is not a religious work, it is a spiritual work. It sets forth a simple and truth-filled idea that many of us grapple with: we are each and all unconditionally loved by God. And since we are each and all unconditionally loved by God, ***we are each and all lovable***.

Allow this book to teach you not to rely on others for your sense of value or self-worth. You are inherently valuable—your worth is intrinsic, it was built in when God created you.

Allow this book to take you a step further into a new way of looking at God: as your lover. Certainly not as a romantic lover; God is not your romantic partner, and this book makes no assertions to that effect. The statement **God is in love with you** means God loves you unconditionally and fully, without reservation, hesitation, condemnation, deprivation, or expectation.

Reading this book requires only three things of you:

1.   **Openness**—be open to what is stated here, be open to a new way of thinking and being.

2.   **Acceptance**—be willing to accept what you read when and if it resonates with you.

3.   **Practice**—practice infusing all you do with love, compassion, and kindness. This becomes easier and easier as you realize the unfathomable depths of God's love, which dwells at the center of your being.

Thank you for reading this book, and may you know the love of God more fully and radiate it more beautifully to everyone in your world.

Namaste, Valerie Love

Love

"But anyone who does not love does not know
God—for God is love."
1 John 4:8 (NLT)

"God is love; and he who dwells in love abides
in God."
1 John 4:16 (NLT)

God is love. God *is* love.

The first time I read this passage of scripture must have been more than thirty years ago, and I've read it hundreds of times since. I must confess, my tiny human mind still doesn't fully understand it. It is beyond my thinking faculty to fathom how God could *be* love.

There are concepts we don't understand from a purely mental stance that we have little problem understanding from the spiritual perspective. We are human and spiritual beings at once, and capable of ascertaining spiritual truths that

stump the human mind. The feeling we get inside speaks for itself. When we read the passage
of scripture that states, "God is love," we may not
fully grasp it on an intellectual level and, thankfully, we don't have to. Something deep within
us understands it and, more than that, *knows it
to be true*.

Your life may not appear to be a shining example of the truth that God is love. You may have
experienced horrific circumstances or situations.
You may be living in pain right now. All I ask is
for you to read on and take one step at a time.
Remember, **God is love**. You know this already
deep within; you were born knowing it.

Operate today from the powerful position of
knowing God as love within you. This Love has
always been there, right at your core. God loves
you so much and is willing to do *anything* to get
your attention, so that you may come to learn
the truth of who God is in you and the truth of
who you are. You may be stripped of possessions, or people, or jobs, or good health. None
of it matters. All such things are transitory and
migratory. People and things transition in and
out of our lives spontaneously—accept this and
live happy. Some people migrate out of our lives
and find their way back again—accept this too
and live happy. It is not strange or unusual for

you to experience pain, loss, and suffering; every human being on the surface of the earth has experienced or will experience all these and more.

The most important concept to remember today is that God is *always* with you, in you, and surrounding you. You are always and continuously enveloped in Love. You are never alone. Unlike people, it is not possible for God to transition out of your life or to migrate away from you.

Read this affirmation slowly and repeatedly:

Any experience you have in which you are tempted to believe God is not present is simply an invitation for you to open yourself to Love and to experience how close God truly is, in that moment, even in the midst of what seems to be an ungodlike situation. The more unlike God your situation is, the greater your opportunity to learn, grow, and transform.

This is the eternal challenge of our human nature: to see what is not visible to human eyes. To see God even when everything around us looks to be the opposite of God. To see peace where there seems to be no peace. To see love where there seems to be no love. To see compassion and kindness where neither seems to be. When you begin to understand what is happening in your life and why, and that every challenge is a gift—another chance to see God in action—you'll begin to know God is always with you, in you, and surrounding you.

God is love.

Thoughts for Today

God is love.

God is love in me.

I know God's love is within me, surrounding me, and working through me.

God's love enfolds, envelops, and enlivens me.

I am the love of God made manifest. I see love and compassion where there seem to be none.

I am compassion.

I am love.

Amen.

Omnipresence

"The Lord is with me, I will not be afraid . . ."
Psalms 118:6 (GNT)

"I look above me, below me, around me, within
me, and all I see is God. God is all there is."
John Randolph Price, *Practical Spirituality*

There ain't a place God ain't. God is in the
crack house. God is in the whorehouse. God is in
the jailhouse. God is in the outhouse. There ain't
a place God ain't. God is in the morgue. God is in
the funeral home. God is at the cemetery.
There ain't a place God ain't.
God is in the operating room.
God is in the neonatal intensive care unit.
God is in the intensive care unit.
There ain't a place God ain't.
God is in the bum on the street.
God is in the hooker.
God is in the drug addict.

There ain't a place God ain't.
God is in the murderer.
God is on death row.
God is in the electric chair.
There ain't a place God ain't.
God is in you.

You are a living, moving, breathing expression of God. Act like it. Act like you know God is within you. Own up to your true identity as a divine being who is powerfully creative. Act like you know who you are. Act in accordance with your divine nature.

The beauty about God being everywhere is that God is with you and in you everywhere you go, and can touch your heart at any moment. God is not afraid of the crack house or the jailhouse. God is not tempted at the whorehouse. God is anywhere you are, wherever that may be.

We have been taught to believe that God is not in certain places; that some places are not holy and therefore cannot welcome the presence of God.

While it is true that some places seem holier than others, it is also true that God is everywhere, in all, through all, surrounding all. When you go to a church or temple or mosque, you may be able to feel God's presence immediately upon entering.

Does this mean that God is in some places and not others? No.

The difference between the mosque or temple or church and the whorehouse is that the former are open to God's presence, recognize it, acknowledge it, and act accordingly whereas in the latter, God's presence has not been acknowledged, and the people there act out of harmony with God's presence and their own divine nature.

Just because God's presence is ignored doesn't mean it isn't there. You can ignore gravity by jumping off a building—that doesn't make gravity go away. You can ignore a warning that fire is hot by putting your hand in it—you'll still be burned.

Some of us are aware of God's presence within us. We acknowledge it and act in accord with our divine nature, which causes life to proceed well.

Some ignore God's presence in their lives and act out of accord with their own divine nature, and life becomes full of pain, worry, fear, and suffering.

You have a choice.

You can move forward in the world with the awareness that God is present everywhere you are, and act in accord with that awareness. As a result, your life will begin to reflect awareness of God's presence by becoming more peaceful, purposeful, joyful, fulfilled, inspired, loving, and compassionate.

You can act without awareness of God's presence and reap the consequences that come from ignoring God.

Ignoring God doesn't make God go away.

Not believing in God doesn't make God any less present.

That is one of the many beauties of the universe: God is present everywhere, at all times. You can't leave home without God.

Today, no matter where you find yourself throughout the day, make the conscious decision to act as if you remember and know that God is right where you are, in each and every instant. Make the choice to move today with God as your guide. Make the choice to listen quietly for God's guidance from within your soul when faced with decisions or perplexities.

Know that God is with you, in you, surrounding you, and seeks to express as you always and in all ways.

As you do, you'll see that each day holds a miracle waiting to unfold, just for you.

God is right where you are.

Thoughts for Today

Today I am aware that God is right where I am.

I know and feel God's presence within me in every place, situation, and circumstance.

I act in harmonious accord with my divine nature.

I feel the loving presence of my Creator wherever I go.

I am ever present to God's love.

I am thankful God is right where I am.

Perfect

"So God created man in His own image, in the
image and likeness of God He created him; male
and female He created them."
Genesis 1:27 (AMP)

"And God saw everything that He had made,
and behold, it was very good and He approved it
completely."
Genesis 1:31 (AMP)

God created you in unimaginable love. And
after you were formed, God called you exceed-
ingly beautiful. God called the new creation, humans, very good. You are approved of fully and
completely.

The question is: Do you approve of yourself
fully and completely?

God brought you into existence to become
manifest in an entirely new and different way
than ever before. God created you by bringing

into existence an individual who was completely new, someone the world had never seen before, and would never see again. God desired to create someone who would serve a very unique purpose here; someone who would fill a unique position in the scheme of all creation.

That unique someone is YOU.

Yes, God's great and limitless imagination went to work on a blank canvas conjuring up greatness. You became the masterpiece God created.

When you were fashioned, God thought of what kind of person you would be, what you would do for the world, and what you would look like. No detail was left unplanned, including your beautiful hair and eyes, with their perfect texture and color. Love gave you a body that would serve you well for the purpose you were called into human existence to fulfill. You received the perfect skin color and body size and shape to make manifest your Creator on earth in a completely new and different way.

Contrary to what you may have been told, or conditioned to believe:

You are the perfect size.

Your butt is not too big.

Your nose is not too long.

Your penis is the perfect size.

Your boobs are just perfect for you.
Your hair is the right color and texture.
Your wrinkles make you look wise.
You're not too fat or too skinny.
Your gray hair is distinctive.
Your skin is the perfect color.
Your eyes are amazing windows to your soul.
You are perfect just the way you are.
You are perfect just the way you are.
If you're like me, this may be a difficult con-
cept to wrap your mind around, but you must if
you are to live God's purpose for your life. I've
been told that my nose is too big for my face.
I've been told that my size-eleven-wide feet are
enormous for a woman of my stature. I've been
told, subliminally and overtly, so many negative
notions about my body that one book does not
suffice to put it all in writing.

You've probably been told quite a few unflat-
tering things about the way you look as well, or
you may have picked up some bizarre ideas of
what beauty is from your environment or culture. The truthfulness of these ideas of beauty
or handsomeness usually go unquestioned; we
accept them as fact. The truth is: all the beauty
or handsomeness in the world that you need to
know about is staring right back at you every
time you look in the mirror. From this day for-

ward, there's no reason for you to believe in anyone else's standard of what's beautiful, especially if that standard conflicts with what you look like.

Even when what we look like does not fit our idea of what we want to look like, we are still perfect, just the way we are right now. Perfect lessons are unfolding. Learn them well. Then move on.

Furthermore, if there are aspects of your appearance you don't like, and that are within your control to change, by all means, make *healthy* changes that support you. These healthy changes may include a more nutritious diet, taking vitamins or minerals, drinking more water, exercising more often, or thinking more healthful thoughts. Improving the health and functioning of your body is a way to show honor and appreciation for the magnificent human temple you presently inhabit.

However, our society has become obsessed with changing appearances to conform to some strange idea of beauty, causing the cosmetic surgery industry to boom. Folks want bigger breasts, butt implants, smaller noses, higher cheekbones, flatter tummies, tighter skin, et cetera, et cetera, et cetera. That game can go on and on—we may even know or have heard of folks who have had surgery after surgery and still aren't happy with their appearance. When does it end? When do we look in the mirror and say to ourselves emphatically:

I am perfect just the way I am right now! God made me perfect!

All success in improving our lives begins with one critical element: self-love. If we cannot love and accept ourselves at this very moment, whatever we look like, how can we love ourselves to the place where we would like to be?

Self-love is not a luxury—it's a necessity for healthful living.

So, if no one has ever told you before, let me be the first to say to you:

You're perfect just the way you are!

I don't need to know what you look like to be able to make this affirmation concerning you. What you look like on the outside is simply the clothing God wrapped your soul in when you came here. Always remember God wrapped your soul in the perfect shell when you were born, regardless of what that shell looks like; everything God does has purpose and design. We have placed so much value on (or have devalued) what we look like, that we've forgotten our appearance has nothing to do with who we really are: magnificent, unique, one-of-a-kind creations of an all-loving God.

Your value doesn't come from what you look like.

With that said, because Love created you as a unique, one-of-a-kind, artistic expression, you are *inherently* valuable. After all, Picasso, Rembrandt, and others have created one-of-a-kind artistic expressions of their own design, some of which are worth millions. Are you not more valuable than a painting on canvas?

A wise man once said that God feeds the birds of heaven and clothes the lilies of the field in beautiful adornment. If God would go to such great lengths to feed wild birds and adorn wild flowers, how much more would Love do for you?

It is necessary to your growth that you begin understanding your intrinsic value. You're valuable just because you're here. God made you and you have a right to be here and to be the embodiment of perfection God created you to be. There are no accidents; therefore, you could not have been an accident, regardless of what you may have been told. Every one of us, including you, is a unique, perfect, intentional, one-of-a-kind designer original by God Almighty. This is true whether your natural parents welcomed your birth or not.

You must grow to understand that you are a unique treasure made by God's own creative hand. Just as an artist expresses herself through her work, God is expressing through you. The book of Genesis says that God called the new creation—humans—very good. When God created you, all heavenly creation rejoiced.

Thoughts for Today

Today I know and honor myself as a one-of-a-kind, unique expression of God's love.

God is love and because I am made in the image and likeness of the Creator, I am love.

I am perfect, just the way I am, in this very moment.

My value doesn't come from how I look, or what I wear, or how I speak, or where I live or work, or from anything I've done.

My value is inherent and intrinsic.

I am valuable because I am.

I am a love child.

I am priceless.

Purpose

"Many plans are in a man's mind, but it is the Lord's purpose for him that will stand."
Proverbs 19:21 (AMP)

"I want to say without hesitation that the purpose of our life is happiness."
His Holiness the Dalai Lama

Not only were you called forth in unimaginable love, but God had a specific reason for doing so. You are here to participate in a four-part purpose:

Part 1: You are here to *be*. Consider this: at this very moment, there's nothing you have to do. You are a human *being*, not a human *doing*. To *be* means we understand deep within our core that we are enough, just as we are right now. As we've already seen, we are perfect, magnificent creations of a perfect Creator.

What does that mean? It means you're not here to fulfill anyone else's expectations, demands, requests, solicitations, goals, ambitions, hopes, or dreams.

You are here to *be* the fullest expression of who God created you to be. That's it. Simply be.

What does it mean to simply *be?* At one time you knew what this meant, but since you may have forgotten, find a small infant to observe. They are the best examples I can think of to illustrate the concept of *being*. The happiest people on earth are babies because they instinctively know they have no job to do, no function to fulfill, no responsibilities to see to, no expectations to live up to, no requirements to meet. When you were a baby, there was no pressure on you to do anything. No one expects a baby to do anything but lay there and be cute. Babies are happy in the skin they're in, just enjoying life. Simply *being*. They resonate with this powerful truth because they're unadulterated in their connection to the Source from whence they've just emerged, from the world of Spirit, from God's very bosom.

A critical first step in experiencing true fulfillment and happiness in living your purpose is to resonate with this simple truth, just as a baby does: we are human *beings*. God didn't give you a to-do list when you emerged from your mother's womb. When you were born, God didn't put an in-box beside you.

I must warn you: this path is simple, yet far from easy. Learning who you really are and knowing it is enough may be one of the most challenging principles you learn to master.

Sit still for a moment. Do nothing. Let this simple truth sink in: before you *do* anything, master learning how to simply *be*.

Understand this: no more is required of you other than being the best person you can be in each God-given moment. When we internalize the principle of *being*, rather than *doing*, we enter bliss. If we sit in stillness and give no heed to anything or anyone else, we will have found one of the most elusive jewels men search for: perfection. Perfection is elusive because we search for it externally, when it actually resides within each one of us. *A Course in Miracles* accurately states:

"There is a place in you where there is perfect peace. There is a place in you where nothing is impossible. There is a place in you where the strength of God abides."

The only way to find that perfect place inside of you is to just be. You won't find that perfect inner stillness by running around, going here and there, rushing this way and that. You only find that perfect place when you sit in the stillness and decide to just *be*. Develop a practice of sitting in stillness and silence and doing nothing. Just *be*. God created a special day for us to just be—it's called the Sabbath. It is a holy day of rest and relaxation, a day to practice doing nothing. It is the delicious pause that your mind and body need to connect with your Love within.

There is a positive side effect, among many, of learning to just *be*. You will no longer give more consideration to what other people think of you than you do to your own inner voice of wisdom (more on this in a later chapter). This is quite liberating, because listening to our inner voice of wisdom informs us that the answer to every question lies within ourselves, and the infinite wellspring of wisdom each of us searches for actually resides in our core.

Part 2: You are here to be happy. If you haven't noticed, God is pretty happy. If you'll gaze at your life and surroundings, you'll probably find evidence of God's sense of humor. Animals, plants, and humans are quite funny, and may even be funny looking.

God wants you to be happy, joyful, and fulfilled. It is our natural state to be happy and to want happiness for every person we love. There is a natural slant in the Universe toward happiness, a natural bias for joy. Your default setting is happiness and well-being.

Why, then, if it is our natural state to be happy, are most of us so unhappy?

The reason for the rampant, widespread dissatisfaction and unhappiness with life that most people experience is connected to what was stated earlier in this book: not realizing who God is and who we really are. If we fully accept and know God as Love within us and working through us, and that we are unconditionally loved, and that we are perfect and whole, unique creations, valued and valuable, and that every soul on earth is too, would there ever be any reason to be unhappy? When we know, on a very deep level, that we are one with Love, and one with everyone and everything in creation, we become happy.

Our being happy does not mean we suffer no challenges in life. There may be challenges, yet when we remember the truth of who God is and the truth of who we are, we always find our way back to happiness, which is our natural state. Yes, happiness and joy are your default settings.

However, when challenges arise, we tend to forget God is within us, with us, and working

through us. We tend to forget we are unconditionally loved and thus would never be subjected
to anything that would completely destroy us.
We tend to forget we are perfect and unique creative expressions of God.

Because we can so easily contract amnesia,
we become unhappy. I can contract amnesia on
a moment-by-moment basis. I can be happy in
the knowledge of who God is and who I am in
this moment, but if my husband or one of my
children decides to say something I find objec-
tionable, I may forget. For a split second, I may
forget who God is and who I am.

Thankfully, God knows we are forgetful, so
there are always reminders along life's path that,
anytime we get off course, snap us back to the
happiness state of being. Unfortunately, most of
us are too preoccupied with *doing* (rather than
being) that we don't notice God's gentle but sub-
tle reminders along the way that all is well, and
that all things work together for our good. When
we do notice the reminders of happiness God
places along the way, life becomes very exciting.

For instance, have you ever noticed that right
in the middle of being angry with someone, something strangely funny may happen to you? A kid
may say something that makes you want to fall out
on the floor laughing? Or you look down and see

that in your haste, anger, and inattention you managed to put on two different shoes, and now you're out the door on your way to work? Or you may read a billboard or a car license plate that gives you a message you needed? All of these incidents are God's way of reminding you to be happy. Are you paying attention?

I recall one such incident my husband and I experienced. We were coming out of a restaurant one night, after having a lovely meal, and got into a disagreement about something. The funny thing is, I have no recollection of what the disagreement was about in the first place. Anyway, as we were leaving the restaurant, it was clear that we were both very heated. We were heading to our car to drive home when a man approached us out of nowhere in the parking lot and asked for a ride home. We both looked at him strangely, not because of his request, but because of our own internal states of mind. I wanted to say, "You want a ride? Can't you see that we aren't very happy now? Here we are, minding our business, having a perfectly good argument, and here you come disturbing us!" My husband was not inclined to give him a ride, and neither was I. I was thinking about the nerve of this man to interrupt me just as I was about to make the argument's winning point that would surely prove to my husband, once and for all, that I was right.

But the man was insistent. He kept trying to convince us, and wouldn't go away. We sensed no danger from him, and he lived close by, so we acquiesced. As we were riding, the man decided to engage us in light conversation about being happy in each moment, and that life doesn't last forever, so you best make each day count. He talked about looking at life from a positive viewpoint, and not letting anything change that perspective. He was lighthearted and uplifting. When he got out, we watched as he approached the house he said he lived in. Then he disappeared. We never saw a door open. He just vanished.

The most interesting aspect of this story was how we both felt when the man left. We were no longer arguing, and the entire mood in the car had changed from argumentative, combative, and angry, to calm and contemplative. My husband and I had both been turned around from an angry state of mind that was not natural to us, to one that was closer to our natural, default state: happiness and joy.

Part 3: You are here to be happy on purpose. To be happy on purpose is to have discovered our specific and unique gifts, talents, and abilities, and to have applied them successfully to life in such a manner that our existence becomes effortless, joyful, fulfilled, and abundant. In order to discover successfully the highest and best use of our gifts, talents, and abilities, a good amount of soul-searching is in order. But let me warn you in advance: this work is not for the faint-hearted. In the words of my good friend Nicole's mother, "Growing up and getting older ain't for sissies." Going inward, to the depths of one's soul, can be the most frightening and daunting, albeit necessary, journey any one of us can take. Courage is in order. Thankfully, we have help.

The assistance we need for this process to properly unfold comes to us when we consider, once again, our genesis. We emanated from the Source of all divine power and love. The Creator formed each one of us with a specific and unique mission in mind. Before we were brought here, we were imbued with everything we would ever need to walk our individualized path successfully. The beauty in all of this is that God's purpose for us and our soul's true desire are perfectly aligned. Thus, not only are we impeccably suited for our specialized mission, it is also the path that makes our heart sing. There is a passion burning inside you to live the life for which you were commissioned and especially created!

Let's go back to our example of the artist. Dale Chihuly is one of my favorite artists. What he is able to create with blown glass is beyond words, mental comprehension, or ability to describe in any way. I gaze at his work with awe, and I've witnessed countless others doing the same. Since he's an internationally renowned artist, he's frequently commissioned to create special works of art for certain public spaces. When he's commissioned to do a work of art, naturally, the price is set in advance and is high. The reason he can command large sums of money for his artwork (before he's even created it) is because he's a proven artist. The folks who are hiring him know his work and what he is capable of creating. They know his work to be breathtaking, and that what he'll create for them is likely to be breathtaking as well. You've probably seen his works of art in high-end hotels and casinos, or in museums. When the request is made for him to create a special piece, he is shown where the work of art will go and what purpose it will serve. He then creates a magnificent piece of art that will perfectly fit the space and mood.

God is the greatest artist of all time, and you would benefit from considering yourself as being infinitely more valuable than made-to-order, commissioned artwork. The Great Artist's work is well known. You fit perfectly with God's design, and you are important. You were made to fill a space only you can fill. You are much more valuable than any one-of-a-kind commissioned work of art. You can never be duplicated. Just as a commissioned work of art has a space prepared for it in advance, you too have an important space prepared for you in advance, and the world is waiting for you to take your rightful place in it. No one else will do, for no one else can or could fill your space. Only you can. Will you?

Part 4: You are here to be happy on purpose in service. There's one simple question which will make us strive for excellence while we are here: how is the world made better because I am here? Working backwards from the answer to that question will help us determine how to live on a daily basis.

What is your personal contribution to the world around you? How are you serving others? The keys to your happiness lie in the answers.

Two great examples of this concept of service to others are Jesus Christ and Buddha.

Jesus' positive imprint on the world remains immeasurable. Many feel the world was made better because He walked here, and I concur. Jesus exemplified all four aspects of why He

was created and brought forth. He understood
deeply the concept of just *being*. He practiced
it on several occasions, disappearing into the
wilderness to simply be. His deeply compassionate heart enabled him to reflect pure happiness
and joy. He understood his special and unique
talents, gifts, and abilities and used them to the
fullest extent humanly and supernaturally possible to aid others. His disposition was that of a
servant rather than a king. On two occasions, He
stooped to wash the feet of his comrades, thus
illustrating the prime importance of service to
others. He actively sought ways to help others,
and succeeded every time. Jesus knew well His
purpose and commission, and lived it boldly,
without apology. In His life and His death, Jesus
Christ was the very embodiment of living one's
purpose.

Indeed, Christ knew how to be happy on purpose in service.

Another superb example of an extraordinary
life lived in service to others is that of Buddha.
The positive impact his life has had on billions of
people around the world is undeniable. Though
his life started off pampered and protected,
when he learned the painful state of the world
outside his sheltered existence, he immediately
left on a search for life's meaning. After many

years, he reached enlightenment, and returned home to aid his family in their search for truth and meaning. Not only did Buddha help his family reach enlightenment, he also became a guide to enlightenment for countless others during his earth walk. He remains a powerful force for personal transformation to millions worldwide. Buddha's life exemplified being happy in service to others.

What about your life? What has your life exemplified up to this point? If you've been an outstanding example of service to others, excellent! If you have work to do in that arena, don't verbally or mentally punish yourself for what you didn't do yesterday, just vow to do something different right now. Vow now to be better. Vow now to make the world better because you're here. Vow now to take your rightful place in the circle of life and be happy on purpose in service.

In the popular movie *The Lion King*, Simba learns, through a series of trials and happenings, to take his rightful place as king of Pride Rock. He learns to do his part to ensure the circle of life as intended by nature. At one point, he runs off (after experiencing the devastating death of his father) to live a carefree existence with those who have no goals in life other than getting the next meal of bugs and worms. Meanwhile, back at Simba's home, life without balance soon becomes chaotic, and because the delicate circle of life has been upset, destruction ensues. In the natural order of things in the jungle, the lion is king of beasts, not the hyena. A messenger, Rafiki, comes to Simba to remind him of his rightful place as king. Rafiki tells Simba pointedly, "You don't even know who you are." Pretending to be a warthog when you're really king of the jungle doesn't work. Simba was not being authentic, so his life wasn't fulfilled. After his late father, Mufasa, communicates with him from the spirit world, Simba is able to recall his power and his legacy as heir to the throne. He is able to remember *who he really is*.

I refer to this story because it so accurately depicts our human journey. We experience pain, loss, suffering, or hardship and we run and hide. We forget who we really are. We deny our power, or we choose to give it away. We decide to live a carefree life with folks who do not encourage us to be or do anything great. After all, they have a vested interest in us staying small and unfulfilled: that way, they get to stay small and unfulfilled. We do all this running, hiding, and denying because we think it's easier than the alternative: being ac-countable and owning our power. Being accountable, owning our power, and living up to our God-given potential exacts something of us: it requires us to overcome challenge after challenge to rise higher and higher; it requires us to feel the pain and push through it to the lesson and the blessing that are surely on the other side; it requires us to be the best we can be in every way in every moment; it requires dirty work. And let's face it: some of us don't want to get dirty.

Yet, if we're to have complete fulfillment and come to know joy and happiness sublime, we must joyfully decide to live our lives on purpose, and walk the path God laid out for us before we came here, no matter how dirty it requires us to get.

The purpose for which God created you is simple, though it may not always be easy. As I've stated, it can be a difficult road to traverse, with many perils along the way. Despite the hardships and perils along the path, it's one we are drawn to walk if we are to be completely and utterly content.

Understand and practice simply being—being the best person you can be. This requires learning the art of doing nothing; learning to sit in stillness and just *be*. From this state of perfect *being*, there arises within us a deep and profound happiness; which sets the stage for us to do the internal work necessary to discover our unique talents, skills, abilities, and passions. You'll then be able to use these discoveries in meaningful and practical service to others so as to enrich their lives, and your own as well. Remember this: the world's pain and sadness are remedied by your unique gifts and how you choose to apply them to those who are in need of your help. It will be your pleasure to serve them.

This profound quote from Frederick Buechner illumines just how happy we are to be living our purpose when we get up enough nerve to do it: *"The place where God calls you is the place where your deep gladness and the world's deep hunger meet."*

You are here to live on purpose and to fill a unique and important place in the grand design that only you can.

God created you to be happy on purpose in service.

Thoughts for Today

*Today I know God created me for a purpose;
and I assume my important and unique place
in the grand design.*

*I am an heir and it is God's good pleasure to
give me the Kingdom.*

*I live each day on purpose—doing what I love
in service to others.*

*Because I live my life on purpose, my life flows
from day to day smoothly, abundantly, and
joyfully.*

I am sublimely happy and infinitely fulfilled.

Life in my world is very good!

Create

"For as he thinks in his heart, so is he."
Proverbs 23:7 (AMP)

"By the cumulative, distilled essence of your
mentality at any given moment, you draw to
yourself all that manifests in your life."
Eric Butterworth, *The Universe is Calling*

God designed us with an internal creative power. We have the ability, using this power, to create any reality we desire. This power is at work always, even when we're not aware of it.

This point is worthy of repetition: You are always in a creative process, even when you aren't consciously aware of your creative power and ability. This internal creative power is limitless in its potential, and is *always* active within each of us.

This creative power is your pattern of thinking, which escalates to your beliefs.

Your most dominant thoughts, which become your beliefs, create your reality.

Consciousness creates.

Though we may blame others for our undesirable experiences, the creative power truly rests in one place and one place only: the six inches between our ears. In other words, if you have undesirable conditions in your life right now, the origin of these effects lies in your consistent and persistent pattern of thinking. Likewise, any desirable life conditions you currently enjoy can also be accredited to one thing: your consistent and persistent pattern of thinking.

Everything in our existence flows from thought, which starts in the invisible realm and becomes manifest in physical form. There is an invisible forerunner and counterpart to every manifest action, situation, and circumstance. Everything first occurs in the invisible realm of thought, desire, and belief, and later becomes manifest in the visible world of form and matter.

It is a law of the Universe: the law of cause and effect.

This is the creative process. God used (and uses) this creative process to bring everything into existence: God first held in mind the potential creation, then spoke the idea aloud, after which it appeared in the manifest world.

This remains the only creative process and the only means by which anything can enter the world of form: by first being created in the invisible realm of thought, belief, and desire.

Your most dominant thought patterns have created, and are continuing to create, everything you currently have in your world.

This principle applies to *everything* in your world, even unwanted and undesirable conditions. The unfortunate part of this equation is that we rarely believe we are responsible for creating even a fraction of the mayhem in our lives: some of us act like victims, when, in reality, we are powerful creators.

The fact that I create my experience was one of the hardest lessons for me to learn. I was a champion victim. "Look what happened to me now!" and "Why do these kinds of things always happen to me?" were the sorts of thoughts I frequently entertained.

I've learned now that it is more useful to me in my spiritual progress to ask: "How, and more importantly, why, did I create this experience?" "If I find that I continually create the same kinds of experiences for myself (such as abuse, addiction, anger, poverty, and lack, or anything else undesirable) what are the lessons I need to learn so I can move on?"

It takes absolute guts and courage to own up to our nasty creations. It's easier, in the beginning, to run, hide, and play victim. It's easier, in the beginning, to find a scapegoat or to insist someone else did this to us, rather than realizing that something in our own internal world drew that experience to us. No experience that happens on the physical plane of existence can occur unless it was first magnetized by the internal condition. Our internal states of being—mental, emotional, and spiritual—are the playgrounds of creation.

Creation follows an orderly process in every respect and aspect; we do not live in a random, chaotic, disorderly system. We've already seen God's creative process: a creative idea held in mind with a powerful intention (and with great love), followed by the spoken word and accompanied by action leads to manifestation. Our creation process is identical: first we think it, then we feel it, then we usually speak it, then we act accordingly, which leads to manifestation in the physical world.

You can fight this concept, or you can agree with it. It's completely your choice. Whatever you decide, the creation process is proceeding in your life according to spiritual law, whether you choose to work with the spiritual law or not.

Just because one chooses not to accept or work within spiritual law doesn't mean the law is not operative. Gravity doesn't need your belief or agreement in order to do what it does.

I had great resistance to this concept when I first learned how spiritual law operates, and I find that many who come to my retreats and workshops have resistance to it as well. Some of us have chosen, on quite a few occasions, to be victims—thinking we've gotten off the hook by way of blame. It's her fault. It's his fault. It's the dog's fault.

How about a new approach? How about looking in the mirror and honestly saying, "I created this mess. Now I choose to create something different—something I like better than this."

Realizing that you create your experience bit by bit in every single moment through your thoughts, intentions, feelings, decisions, words, and actions can be disheartening if what you've created up to this point has been undesirable. After all, who would create an abusive relationship, or addiction, or divorce, or depression, or any of life's situations we call ugly?

You would, that's who.

Don't feel alone; I've done it too. And so have countless other folks.

Every person alive has, at some point, created something undesirable. When undesirable creations show up, the origin is most likely a fear (or multiple fears) of what we don't want to happen. If your thoughts of what you *don't* want to happen are stronger than your thoughts of what you *do* want to happen, you'll attract your worst fears.

I once went rock climbing, thinking it would help me with my fear of high places. In the days leading up to the climb and while physically preparing for the climb, I had one major fear: the fear of falling. As I strapped up my equipment, my palms got sweatier and sweatier. My heart raced. My muscles tensed as adrenaline coursed through my body. When it was my turn to start the climb, my knees were shaking so badly I could barely steady myself. All the while, the fear of falling was driving my every move. What do you suppose happened? Yes, within a few moves up the rock face, I fell. The protective gear kept me from getting hurt. I was okay physically, though I was quite shaken emotionally. A noticeable shift occurred after I calmed down: I no longer dreaded falling. After all, I had fallen and I had survived. I continued the climb without the overwhelming sense of fear I'd had earlier. That fear had been met and successfully overcome.

The fall was probably the best thing that could've happened to me.

There is an alternative. We don't have to create situations from a place of fear. When you give more consideration to what you fear than to what you desire, what you fear will show up every time. Your mental energies are focused on what you don't want. Then you wind up creating in your experience what you don't want because that was the strongest and most dominant thought pattern in your psyche, and the strongest emotion you were emitting.

Most of us unconsciously create from a place of fear, and thus attract all sorts of negative and destructive situations, circumstances, and even people.

If you morbidly fear getting cancer, and that thought is dominant, and the fearful feeling attached to it is stronger than the desire to be healthy and the grateful feeling you have for your good health, then you're making it easier for cancer to set up residence in your physical body.

If you're a fearful driver, you'll probably be in more car accidents than a careful, confident driver. You'll attract to yourself car accidents because you drive in a constant state of fear (even if subconsciously) about having a car accident.

Take a moment now to look around at all the negative conditions, circumstances, or people in your world. How did each one get there? Did you have a hand in creating any of it? If your answer is yes, then you're taking responsibility and can grow from your acknowledgement. If your answer is "No, I'm not responsible for any of it," then you're likely to land in the same unwanted predicaments over and over, because you've not owned your share in the creative process. When you play the victim, you're powerless. When you stand as the creator you know yourself to be, you are powerful beyond human ability.

Abusive relationships abound. This is an area in which one party is usually referred to as the perpetrator and the other party is cast as the victim. Might it be that both parties have a hand in the creative process? Can there be an abusive relationship between two people without both parties? We are not called upon to answer for others and their actions, but we are accountable for our own. The question to ask is: how does one attract an abusive partner? There are multiple beliefs operating in the psyche of the abused partner, including: feeling that the abuse is somehow warranted or deserved; a need to be punished; not knowing how to—or being able to—create and maintain clear boundaries. Low self-esteem is also likely present.

Abuse cannot survive in the presence of love. No one would ever again be in an abusive relationship if the love of God were remembered and emanated. The more we remember God's unconditional love, the more loving our world becomes. With a consistent and persistent thought pattern of God's unconditional love, we attract loving relationships.

Taking responsibility for what you create is the only way you'll take the internal leap from being a victim to being a powerful creator. Can you take responsibility when the store clerk is rude? Or when she yells? Or when you feel attacked or betrayed? It's all consciousness, and consciousness creates.

We are each powerful creators from birth; it's an inborn natural ability of humans to be able to create whatever life experience suits us. We are made in the image and likeness of God. God is a creator of the highest order. We are each and all powerful creators.

There is another factor in the creation process to be considered. Many of our creations are not devised in the conscious, rational mind, but in the deep, dark recesses of the subconscious mind. The subconscious mind has been conditioned by parents, teachers, friends, culture, society, religion, and the world at large. It is the most powerful computer in existence and contains a record of everything that's ever happened to you, including what you experienced in the womb. The thoughts and beliefs that are alive and active in the subconscious mind will play out in daily life. The beliefs we hold are made manifest in the outer world as conditions.

We can only magnetize to ourselves the dominant thought patterns, beliefs, and desires that are held in our conscious and subconscious states of mind.

The subconscious mind is powerful. It has the ability to heal and destroy. If a belief is present that a doctor can heal disease, the subconscious mind is capable of healing the body whether or not the prescription from the doctor works. The pure and potent belief that a particular cure will work is enough to elicit healing. Doctors have never cured anyone of anything. A doctor has never healed anyone of anything. The only thing which can cure or heal you is your consciousness. This is not a recommendation to not seek medical attention. When medical treatment is called for, it should by all means be utilized. However, know that the medical treatment is there to help cure the body, yet the root cause of whatever ails the body exists in the mind. Until the mind is healed, the body will remain sick and prone to disease.

Many of us have a subconscious mind that is conditioned for lack, scarcity, fear, unworthiness, shame, guilt, and a host of other negative beliefs about ourselves and others. If we're not careful and conscious, much of what we create will arise from our conditioned subconscious mind and could produce negative and unwanted results.

For instance, if the subconscious mind is conditioned for lack because of persistent messages received while growing up in a home where there was never enough, lack will present itself, even though prosperity is truly desired. I grew up in a home where I frequently heard: "money doesn't grow on trees" and "what do I look like to you, Rockefeller?" and "we don't have enough money for that!" As an adult, I replayed lack situations and circumstances for more than twenty years until I came to understand the origin of my experiences: lack and limitation conditioning. Lack and limitation were ingrained in my subconscious, though I consciously declared wealth. A reconditioning of the subconscious mind had to take place before I could begin to experience wealth.

Being abused as a child can create a pattern in the subconscious mind that draws abusive relationships; not because one desires to be drawn into such a relationship, but because that is what one has been programmed to experience.

There is a way to overcome the conditioning and programming of the subconscious mind, and we will address that solution in a later chapter.

In the meantime, accept and own your creative power, realizing and understanding that you create your reality with your thoughts, and that you can re-create your reality anytime you decide to (more on this later too).

If you own your power and step up to being the master creator you truly are, you can experience a completely new and better world!

Exercise: Creatively Manifesting Desires

Create a list of all you truly desire. Write down on several sheets of paper all the dreams and desires you have for yourself. Include your desires for your relationships, your children, and anyone else dear to you. Write down everything that's important to you. Include some fun things you'd like to do also. I undertake this exercise frequently—allowing myself to write freely pages and pages of what I truly desire.

After writing the list, assemble pictures to go along with each statement. Comb magazines and other sources for colorful images that best represent each item you've written down. You'll also need plenty of pictures of yourself. Include pictures of yourself enjoying all you desire.

A great way to use this process is if you think you're overweight. Write down your desired weight and how many pounds you'll release and by when. Write about why you desire to release the pounds and how it will make you feel. Allow yourself to express all the happy, joyful feelings you'll have when you release the extra pounds. Get yourself worked up into a frenzy of appreciation for your new, healthy, happy, and smaller body. Then find a picture of a body in a magazine you think is attractive and that represents how you'd like to look when you reach your ideal weight. Then attach a picture of your head to the body in the picture. Make sure to pick a body that is realistic for you to achieve in the time frame. Then place the picture in a meaningful and prominent place in your home, where you'll see it every day. Taping it to the refrigerator is helpful. You'll be amazed at how your subconscious mind will begin to do the work to create your ideal body. Your work on the physical plane will be much easier, and your weight release plan will work much more successfully. You'll keep pounds off too.

If you want to climb Mt. Everest, get a picture of Mt. Everest and put a picture of yourself on the side of Mt. Everest, or better yet, put yourself on top of Mt. Everest.

I've helped many attendees of my retreats create collages of pictures depicting what they desire in their lives, so that they can begin to be more conscious in their creations. This process works extremely effectively. The reason it does is because pictures and symbols are the language of your subconscious mind. When the mind consistently dwells on pictures or scenes, whether held internally in the imagination or externally on paper, it will do everything in its immense and infinite power to create that scene in physical reality.

If you want to be an excellent public speaker and you hold an image of yourself in your mind successfully speaking to huge, appreciative audiences who are engaged in what you're saying, your mind will get to work immediately to create that reality. It's how athletes and highly successful business people use the power of visualization to achieve astounding results. The mind always seeks to bring into reality the pictures you hold in it. In this way, consciousness creates.

The reason it's so important for you to visualize the best and highest for yourself—or why a collage or collection of photos that feature your desires and you attaining them is so helpful—is because you'll find your mind will latch on to the pictures it sees and immediately get busy creating those scenes for you.

It works like magic.

Your mind has the power to create anything that is consistently held in consciousness.

When you use this power to your benefit, to create what you truly desire, you become a conscious creator rather than an unconscious creator who masquerades as a victim. You'll begin to create what you want according to the desires of your heart, rather than unconsciously attracting to yourself what you fear most.

Use your vast and unlimited creative power wisely; whether you're creating a life you love or a life you struggle through, you're creating. You might as well make it good.

Remember, God is in love with you and you are created in the image and likeness of the Creator.

You are a powerful reality creator.

Thoughts for Today

I am a powerful reality creator.

As such, I choose to create my reality with loving thoughts.

I consistently and persistently hold in consciousness pictures and scenes of a world I desire.

Today, I own my power and create a life filled with the glorious realization of my hopes and dreams.

I am thankful to know myself as the powerful creator of my own reality.

Consciousness creates—I choose to create from love.

Imagine

"Where there is no vision [no redemptive revelation of God], the people perish . . ."
Proverbs 29:18 (AMP)

"When a dream becomes that much a part of you, then it becomes a Vision."
Lazaris, *The Sacred Journey*

My favorite sport when I was little was daydreaming. Some people think daydreaming isn't a sport.

In my childhood daydreams, one minute I was a figure skater performing to the roar of an applauding crowd, the next minute I was slaying strange and wondrous creatures with a long sword, the next minute I was soaring on wings high above the tallest mountain peak.

Never mind that I had never left my classroom.

To me, my daydreams definitely qualified as a sport.

Thankfully, I've never given up daydreaming. I love a good daydream. I still entertain myself with sensational visions dreamed up in my imagination. I take myself to exotic locations all around the world while engaged in the most intriguing and exciting activities . . .

I am in Turkey haggling with the merchants over rugs weaved by hand in the Himalayan Mountains. I go to a Turkish bath and feel the hot water on my skin, followed by the exhilaration of having cold water poured over me from head to toe. . . .

I feel myself lazily gliding down the Venice River in a gondola steered by an Italian donning a red-and-white striped shirt and a wide-brimmed hat. I gaze up and see the underside of the Rialto Bridge as we pass quietly under. I breathe in the aromas of the river. I hear the gentle rustle of waves. I feel the worn wood of the gondola against my palm. . . .

I enter the Louvre museum in Paris, hearing the click of my heels on the marble flooring. I take a crowded elevator up. I work my way through the museum crowd, finally earning a spot in front of the Mona Lisa. *I gaze at her in awe. There's a chemical tinge in the air. I walk and walk and walk and, try as I might, I don't get to see everything in the mammoth structure.*

I go to bed that night reflecting on my day and fall asleep happy, grateful, and satisfied. . . .

I am in the bridge suite at the Atlantis Hotel on Paradise Island in the Bahamas. I greet the white-gloved butler who will attend to my family and me for the week. I run my fingers across the smooth keys of the grand piano. I taste the rich exotic flavors of fresh, sweet island fruit served by our cook just prior to enjoying a meal of fried conch.

Oh yes, my daydreams are definitely a sport!

When I was little, daydreaming was just for fun. Kids imagine anything and everything, frequently and easily. What tends to happen is that adults convince children, in little ways, to shut down their imaginations. I can't count how many times I was told to "stop daydreaming" and come back to the "real world." When I would share the content of one of my particularly exciting daydreams, I remember big people telling me, "Don't be silly; that could never happen." I became accustomed to not talking about my imaginary jaunts, much less speaking of my invisible friends. I couldn't run the risk that they would be dismissed as non-existent by the big people. Somewhere along the way, I reached the point where I didn't share what I saw in the delightful space between my ears—I found solitary delight in keeping it all under wraps.

Now that I'm an adult, I understand why day-dreaming is important, even for grown-ups: it's a starting point from which we create the rich tapestry of life. What we can daydream today, we can experience tomorrow.

Imagination is God's holy gift to us; a gift of love. Imagine what life would be like without the human imagination: no discoveries, no inventions, nothing new. The same old thing day in and day out. Our existence would become so mundane we'd hardly be able to stand it.

Humans long for variety. We long to ask the "what if" questions that fuel the imagination and move the race forward by monumental leaps and bounds.

Imagination plays an essential role in the creation process. There's nothing in my life now—from the new home I've moved into to the vehicle I enjoy driving—that didn't first show up in my imagination. Long before I went to the settlement table to purchase my newest home, I'd seen myself in advance mental previews signing document after document at the real estate closing. Long before I received the physical keys, I'd already felt the cool key-shaped metal being placed in the palm of my hand. And long before I opened the door to my house in the physical realm, I'd mentally rehearsed the event in my imagination.

Imagination is the key to creating a mental picture of what we desire, a necessary step to manifestation on the physical plane. If we have a vivid imagination, we're in position to manifest more of what we desire.

There's no limit to what the mind can cook up. Allow your mind to create scenes you desire to experience. Don't edit yourself. Don't tell yourself that your dreams aren't possible to live. If you can cook it up in your mind, you can live it. Don't ask yourself how it will all come about, and more importantly, don't act like a grown-up!

What you're building is a clear vision for yourself, enjoying your desired experiences in advance of the actual event.

Athletes mentally play winning scenes in advance; whether that means hitting a home run, slamming the ball over the net, making a three-point shot, or running the ball to the end zone. The actual activities differ, yet the process works the same. The practice of visualization is widely used in sports preparation because it works. First an athlete sees it in the mind, then the mind prepares the body to act out the event in an actual game. When an athlete imagines winning, the same muscles in the body that would be used in the actual event respond in the same way to the mind game version of the activity.

The mind is a powerful tool, one of the most powerful you have at your disposal.

Today, be grateful for God's love, which bubbles up from within in the form of imagination. Use the storehouse of power that lies within you. You already have everything you need to get everything you want.

Exercise: Taking Yourself on a Mental Jaunt

Try it now. Put the book down and for the next few minutes, take yourself on a mental jaunt. Imagine going to places that inspire and excite you, with the people you'd love to have along for the ride, having the experiences you'd love to have, with no concern about money or resources. Keep the mental scenes moving. How does it feel? How different would your life be if you exercised your imagination like kids do? What if you treated yourself to a daily daydream break, where you get to live out your heart's desires in full, rich, living color? How much could you dream up for yourself?

The more you imagine yourself in scenes that inspire and excite you, the more you'll begin to pull those experiences out of the mental/emotional realm into the physical realm. It's fairly easy; you've done it hundreds of times. We've all done it. We've all wanted something so badly that we could taste it. We kept it in mind day and night. We thought about it while we ate. We thought about it when we were lying in bed falling asleep. We confided in family and close friends about it. Before long, we were living out the desire in the physical realm. Many of the details we imagine in daydreams actually appear in the physical version of the scene.

God gave you a gift so powerful that you can use it to begin to create anything you desire. Anything. There are no limits to what you can create. There is no one who can censor your daydreams. There is no force that will tell you, "No, you can't have that."

The door is wide open to you. Walk through it.

Thoughts for Today

My imagination takes me to wondrous places.

God has gifted me with the powerful mental tool of imagination—I use it for 'daydream breaks' throughout my day!

My mind shows me possibilities I've never experienced.

My imagination brings me amazing results!

My mind creates my reality—I now make the best reality for myself.

Nothing is impossible for me.

Thank you, God, for the blessing of imagination.

Synchronicity

"If you believe, you will receive whatever you
ask for in prayer."
Matthew 21:22 (GNT)

"Today, through the action of Infinite Intelligence at the center of my being, I am rightly
guided in all my decisions and actions so that
the greatest good comes to me and to others."
Willis Kinnear, *30-Day Mental Diet*

I've given up on planning out my life. I was an
incessant planner, making up elaborate plans and
spreadsheets about what would happen, why it
would happen, and when it had to happen by. I
wasn't doing a particularly great job of it anyway;
so much seemed to come up that wasn't in the
plan. Conversely, much of what was in my elaborate plans didn't seem to play out in real life. After
years of disappointment and discouragement, I
decided I needed to take a different tack. Maybe I

needed to give up so much planning of all the little details of life. Maybe I couldn't plan out every single thing after all. And what was all the planning about anyway? Fear of not being in control?

Just as I began to see I needed to do things differently, the answers came. I learned how to do things differently, which caused different results.

I learned my rightful place, which is stating *what* I truly desire in my life experience and *why* I desire it (or how having that experience would make me feel).

The *how* piece of the equation I've learned to surrender to God.

Here's the process by which our desires and creative ideas manifest:

- A desire or creative idea arises within us from Spirit;
- The desire is fueled with strong emotion, even passion;
- We mentally set an intention that will support the manifestation of the desire, whether or not we realize we are doing this;
- We form and hold mental images of the desire in its fully manifested state while simultaneously sustaining the feeling within us that the fulfilled desire would elicit;

- We waste no mental time or energy on *how* the desire will come about, nor do we waste time or energy on wondering if it will happen and when;
- We put forth action according to the guidance we receive by means of God's Spirit in each moment (called inspired action—more on this later);
- We pray, affirm, and give thanks that it is already done;
- We confidently leave the rest to God, a practice also known as *"let go and let God"*

God gives us the how; all we have to be concerned with is *what* and *why*. The creative ideas and desires we receive from Spirit come in a package: they each contain the means to get themselves completely fulfilled. God doesn't give us half of anything. Your heartfelt desires already have within them the means for being fully fulfilled, in perfect divine order and timing.

If it's that simple, and God already packaged up our heart's desires to be delivered to us, then why isn't everyone experiencing total fulfillment? Everyone's dreams should come true, all the time.

The reason we don't always experience the fulfillment of our heart's desires is because we begin to think, feel, say, and do things that are not in harmonious accord with the desires we hold. This immediately slows down or completely negates their manifestation in our lives. We may experience or create resistance, fear, trepidation, hesitation, or procrastination. When these elements are present, it's not possible for our desires to flow freely to us or through us.

God is not withholding any good thing from you or from me. Christ stated clearly that when we ask—believing that we shall receive—we will receive.

If we don't experience the fullness of God's gifts and blessings in our lives, a sure cause of the problem is our resistance to those blessings. We actually block God's blessings from flowing freely through us into our world by trying to figure out precisely *how* we will get what we want. We don't relinquish control. We don't surrender.

Instead of planning every step of *how* to get what I desire, I've learned to follow the above step-by-step protocol.

It works wondrously. As you'll soon see in full detail, it's the exact process I used to get this book into your hands right now.

After a desire arises within us, we have work to do. The first—and most important—steps to take to fulfill the desire are done in the spiritual, mental, and emotional realms. Physical work is not required at this point in the creation process.

There are two mental steps to engage in at this point: ***The first mental step is to set a clear, passionate intention of what you desire to experience.*** An intention is powerful when it is stated emphatically. Though an intention statement speaks of what we expect to experience from the fulfillment of a desire, it does not speak in terms of attachments to how the desire must manifest. A powerful, emotionally charged and consciously created intention is the starting point of physical manifestation. Since learning the power of intention, I've now taken to focusing my attention on putting forth only intentions that reflect what I truly desire. I invite you to do the same. When we set and state such powerful intentions, forces in the Universe begin to move to bring us exactly what we desire in perfect divine order and perfect divine timing. Nothing happens unless there is a clear, emotionally charged intention leading the way.

Unfortunately, some folks have unknowingly set intentions that bring undesirable results. Other folks don't set intentions for themselves at all, not realizing the creative power of a well-crafted intention statement. Worse yet, some folks don't even know what an intention is—or how effective it can be in the fulfillment of desired experiences—so they're unable to tap into that unseen supernatural force for good. When a clear intention has not been set, it is easy to become sidetracked, distracted, or caught up in the agendas, ideas, and plans of other people. If either of these statements describes you, pay close attention to what's stated here.

The second mental step to engage in at this stage is to form an image of the desire in its fully manifested state. Add as much detail to the mental picture as possible. Practice painting mental pictures of your desires in rich and lavish detail. Make the imagery colorful and vibrantly alive. Add other exciting elements to the scenes, like the people you'd like to have with you or music, if that's important to you. Put yourself in the picture experiencing all the things you desire. Do not watch yourself in your visualizations as if you were an outside third party, looking in on all the fun. See your visualization from the perspective of the first person. Make the scenes dynamic, with moving people and happenings: walk through the scenes and do exactly as you would do in the real-life version. Hold the visualization often and for long periods of time. This requires mental training.

This is where your practice of meditation (spoken of in a later chapter) will assist you in staying in mental control of the images you create.

Most of us have no problem conjuring up mental images of what we don't want, including scary images and scenes. Your meditative practice will condition your mind for good. Once you're able to hold your mental image for seventeen seconds or longer, the Law of Attraction will begin to work on your behalf. Seventeen seconds might not seem like a long period of time, however, your mind can conjure hundreds of thoughts in a matter of seconds. It's no easy feat, for the untrained mind, to hold a mental image of a desirable outcome for seventeen seconds or longer, uninterrupted. Go ahead and try it right now. Don't be dismayed. Keep practicing. You will surely get there. Creating the mental dynamic and moving pictures of what you desire in rich detail is a necessary step in order for you to clearly define what it is you desire, and then to be able to receive it.

The emotional work necessary at this point is to respond to your mental images with the emotions that you would feel if you were actually living out your desire. If the desire's fulfillment would bring you joy, feel the joy *now*. If the desire's fulfillment would bring you peace and tranquility, feel the peace and tranquility *now*. Don't wait. *Feel the good feelings now*. This step will take practice, especially if your usual emotions are not in line with what you desire to feel. This is a critical step as emotion serves as fuel in the creative process. You can't run a car without gas, even if the car is brand new. It will stay completely immobilized without fuel; it won't even turn on. The same is true of you: you remain immobilized without the fuel of passion and emotion that gets your engine running.

Notice that you haven't had to take any physical action yet to bring your desire to fulfillment. You are still doing internal work at this point. If you feel inspired to take a certain action, so be it. Otherwise, continue to work in the invisible realms at this point. Most of us don't do adequate inner work for the big dreams we have. Then we wonder why we get so tired running around doing so much work and things still aren't happening the way we'd like. What's missing? The inner work, the work within your consciousness, is the most important part of the equation. Consciousness creates.

Next, the spiritual work you want to undertake all during the process is to pray. Pray for faith: faith to know that God gives us every good thing. If there's something good we desire but don't yet have, we're somehow blocking it. As soon as we ask, it is already granted by God. So, if we've asked, and we still don't have it, there must be something internally blocking the manifestation of our desire. Our prayer of faith breaks down any barriers that may be present, which impede or completely block our aim. Our faith serves us well at this point if we're currently looking at situations in our lives that are completely opposite of what we desire. For instance, if your desire is for more money, and you're currently experiencing serious lack, you may find it difficult to have full faith that the money you want and need will show up. In this case, your ongoing and continuous prayer for faith will readjust your conscious thinking mind to a state of belief from that of disbelief. When you have a disbelieving state of mind, your prayer work surrounding your desires is like placing a call to the help desk when you have a computer malfunction. For all your faith malfunctions, call God. God is always at the other end of the help line.

Next, start speaking your desire affirmatively, as if it's already done. In another world, it is already done; you just haven't seen it show up yet in your physical existence. Speak positive affirmations all day, every day. The late Catherine Ponder, a prosperity teacher, recommended spending 15 minutes per day to affirm your good and what you desire to happen, out loud. You can even do three sessions that are each five minutes long. Try it and see for yourself the positive impact it has.

Negative affirmations such as: "I can't," "I don't know how," "I wish I could . . ." and "I don't" have a negating influence on our desires.

Having engaged in ongoing internal work toward manifesting your desires, you're now ready to add physical action to the equation. However, it's important here that you remain fully present and open at all times so that you receive the clear guidance you need. This guidance from Spirit will tell you exactly which actions to take and when. You won't have to guess. There's no need to. You have at your disposal a wellspring of guidance and information that is continually bubbling up within you. You need only listen. Then you'll act with clarity and precision. Your efforts and actions will not be wasted. Your energy will not be expended uselessly. You'll use your energy wisely according to how you're being guided in each moment. This will require courage and faith, as some of the things Spirit guides us to do are strange, unfamiliar, or downright terrifying. It's okay—you'll learn as you go.

Let's look at an example of this entire process. Creating a new desire (which happens in the invisible world of thought and emotion as we previously discussed) and utilizing the power of intention is like placing an order for flowers to be delivered. When you place the order, you specify what kind of flowers you are ordering, what kind of vase they'll come in, what you're paying for the flowers, where they will be delivered, and when. When you hang up the phone, you expect the flowers to be delivered on time and in excellent condition, just as you ordered. You may even smile at the thought of receiving the flowers (if you ordered them for yourself), or, if you ordered them for someone else, you may be warmed at the thought of what they may feel when they receive the flowers. It doesn't enter your mind that the flowers won't come. You don't sit up at night and wonder or worry about the flowers and if they'll arrive.

Life works exactly the same way. Whenever we have a desire, we are forming within ourselves a sort of request for something we want. We are, in effect, placing an order. Some of us take more care and time in ordering flowers than we do in ordering our most heartfelt desires.

For example, you may desire a new vehicle; perhaps it's the car of your dreams. Your request is not instantly granted in the physical just because you want it. You must be familiar with and utilize the universal laws, forces, and principles that are at your disposal to bring your desire for a new vehicle to full physical manifestation.

After we've become aware of a desire we have within, we begin to add definition to the desire by giving it more specificity. Your dream car may be a Lexus, or a Mercedes-Benz. You may begin to imagine the style and exterior and interior colors you'd like. You still may not get the vehicle based purely on your visualization, though you're getting closer and closer to physical manifestation.

Here's a trap to be aware of (most people lose the game here): we begin to try to figure out or plan *how* we can obtain it. Most times, it's not clear to us at the very beginning stages how the desire will be fulfilled. Going back to the car example, you may look at your budget and think to yourself that the car of your dreams is way too expensive for you. You then conclude that you won't be able to get the car anytime soon (if at all), because it's way out of your budget. Your dream car has ceased to become a desire for you and has now been demoted to a nice wish. Right then, at that precise moment, it would be helpful for you to remember that you are now minding someone else's business and as a result you will not get what you desire. How is that?

When you begin to think about *how* you'll get the car, you're minding God's business, not your own. Your business is not to figure out *how* you'll get what you want. That's God's business. God is the great Orchestrator of events, people, situations, circumstances, and opportunities. God set this intelligent Universe in motion and all the laws and forces that govern it. One of the supernatural forces at work at all times in God's Universe is synchronicity.

Synchronicity, to me, is the greatest organizing force of the cosmos. It's the unseen power and force that pulls together people, places, events, circumstances, and situations that seem unconnected, yet must align for the mutual benefit of all involved. It's been called coincidence or a random occurrence or just plain old good luck. Understanding our Creator means we understand there are no coincidences or random happenstance events. I'm actually happy to know that God's Universe proceeds according to laws and principles that govern every aspect of life and that maintain order and harmony. It's reassuring to me to know things don't just happen randomly, without rhyme or reason. There's a specific cause to all events and specific laws and principles that govern all events. I rest peacefully knowing that God's laws and principles are always at work.

Synchronicity works because we are all one. When we look about with human eyes, there appear to be different entities, you or me, him or her. However, the truth is, we are one. We are joined in a web of life. When one part of the web moves, or thinks, the whole web is affected. It's how a butterfly can theoretically flap its wings in the U.S., and cause a storm on the other side of the world. This is known as the butterfly effect. The butterfly effect works for us too; just a tiny flap of our creative thought sets in motion a powerful chain of events, seen and unseen.

Synchronicity works closely with the Law of Attraction. As desires arise within us, and as we think and state a powerful intention to claim what we desire, the Law of Attraction is set in motion, bringing to us whatever matches our most dominant and emotionally charged thoughts. While the Law of Attraction brings to us life experiences that match our most dominant thoughts (like attracts like), synchronicity is the force that causes seemingly unconnected people to meet up at precisely the right time for their mutual benefit. Synchronicity is like the engine that keeps the Law of Attraction humming along. Synchronicity is the means and the mode by which the Law of Attraction brings to you the subjects and objects of your most dominant and emotionally charged thoughts.

Synchronicity is God's way of providing the *how* part of the equation for the manifestation of our hearts' desires. For example, have you ever had the desire to do something in service to another human being and somehow the people, resources, and perfect conditions showed up for you, just in time to carry out your good deed? Or have you ever set out to accomplish something and, along the way, all the components you needed started to line up and appear at your door almost by magic? This phenomenon is synchronicity at work.

Synchronicity begins to move for us the second we affirm a powerful intention. This is indeed the first step: defining *what* you want and *why* you want it. In other words, stating what you desire and how that desire would make you feel, or what the experience of living that desire would do for you.

Let's take the example of wanting more money, since this is a common desire. Most people who want more money are still in the state of wanting more money because the focus of their thought is *wanting* more money and not actually *having* more money. As mentioned earlier, we're placing an order each time we come up with a new desire and a matching intention. If your intention is wanting more money, then that's your order and what will be delivered to you is wanting more money, not actually having more money. *Wanting* more money and *having* more money are two distinctly different orders. You won't receive *having* more money when the order you placed was for *wanting* more money. Remember: the laws God set in place govern all life and are immutable, unchangeable, and always at work.

Clearly defining what we want to experience is critical to having it arrive. There's another challenge here. We're usually good at defining what we don't want. Almost everyone I know can offer a long list of things, situations, and circumstances that they don't want. Not many people have clearly and consistently defined all they *do* want to experience. I confess I haven't clarified all my desires in my own mind, which works as a barrier to me experiencing those desires. As long as I'm fuzzy about what I want, what I receive will be equally fuzzy, undefined, and ambiguous.

If you remain unclear on what you *truly* want out of life, with all your heart and soul, God's love can help. How?

God's love abounds such that we are shown a myriad of possibilities every day. If you aren't sure what you want, why not just look around? The more you observe, the more you'll see things that tickle your fancy, and that you might want to experience. This is a world of variety in astonishing array. The beauty of all this variety everywhere around us is that we can try something, and if we don't like it, we can always try something else. Indeed, this is part of the reason we're here, to experience the marvels God placed here for our enjoyment.

For example, let's say you decide you want a change in your line of work. You don't know exactly what you'd like to be doing; you just know you no longer desire to do what you're currently doing. You do know that you have a desire to be more connected to the earth in your daily work. So you decide to try your hand at gardening in your spare time to see if this is an enjoyable activity for you. After working in the garden for a day planting flowers, you find that putting your hands in the earth and coming into contact with bugs and other creatures does nothing for you. However, later in the process, you discover you love the flowers in your garden, and picking and arranging them in a vase brings you utter joy. From this experience you've narrowed down your search and have determined that while you don't relish hanging out with the bugs in the garden, you love working with flowers. The whole exercise was for your benefit and had immense value in getting you to clearly define what you want to do and what would bring you the greatest joy.

Life is just such an experimental playground. Children do it all the time. They try one thing and if they don't like it, they quickly change to something else. If they like that, they'll stay with it for a little while. However, they won't stay on one thing forever—even if it does interest them—simply because they know they've got so many options. Children don't stay stuck because they realize they've got so much more to explore and discover. Be like a child in this regard. Try out things you've never tried before. Discover new things. God put this whole wondrous earth before you in all its stunning beauty for you to enjoy yourself in ever expanding and varied ways. How much of it have you discovered? How much of this earth have you seen? How much of life have you experienced in full, living, vibrant color?

A powerful way to determine clearly and specifically what you want is to experiment. Try new things. Consciously seek new things to learn. In your experiments, you'll find things you love and things you absolutely could do without. It's all good, because it all helps you to determine and more clearly define what elements you truly desire to have in your life. This is one way that you answer the "what" part of the equation.

To give you an example from my own life, I've known, since I was little, that I have a love affair with books. As a child, I was a voracious reader, devouring book after book. I couldn't get enough. I'm still that way. By remembering what I loved doing as a child, I knew my passion had something to do with books, reading, and writing. Through trying out various forms of writing, and by reading and experiencing a wide variety of books, I was able to determine clearly in my mind that I desired and intended to write books that would uplift, inspire, encourage, and contribute to the healing, growth, and transformation of readers. It was through a process of experimentation and elimination that I arrived at my clearly defined writing intention:

Dear God, it is my heartfelt intention to experience fulfillment of my purpose, express my passion, and share my gifts and talents by writing books that serve as a catalyst for healing, growth, and transformation, and that uplift, inspire, engage, encourage, capture, entertain, amuse, teach, and enlighten. Amen!

This intention serves me well as I write. The demonstration of the successful fulfillment of this intention is the book you're now holding.

The same will happen for you when you begin to clearly define what you desire and then state it affirmatively and passionately.

Next, you must answer the "why" part of the equation. Asking yourself why you want a particular experience gives you the opportunity to examine your motives. Why are you doing what you do? Why do you want what you want? What do you intend to accomplish? What do you think you'll experience or feel once the desire has been fulfilled? Who will it impact if you receive your stated desires and intentions? Who will benefit? Answering these questions is almost as important as defining what you want in the first place. In order to become a conscious creator of your reality—which is what this chapter is all about—you'll need to know why you want what you want.

The reason you must define why you want what you want is because your *why* becomes a burning fire within, spurring you on even when the going gets tough. In all accomplishments, there are patches of rough road along the way, where we're faced with what seem like insurmountable obstacles. The huge mountains we sometimes must climb make us wonder if we'll ever actually get what we desire. In these dark and difficult moments, when we are beset with trials on all sides, when nothing seems to be working and when we feel completely overwhelmed and almost ready to give up, our powerful and compelling *why* keeps us moving forward toward full fruition of our hearts' desires.

When we declare that we're going for something, no matter what it might be or how badly we think we want it, opposition to our stated desires and intentions will immediately arise. Opposition can look and feel daunting, yet it is a necessary component in the creation process. Here's how: opposition is the catalyst needed in getting us to become more than we were before. Opposition to our stated desires and intentions is necessary in strengthening our will. When you successfully climb mountains to get what you desire, the exhilaration you feel at the summit is unlike any other feeling. The same feeling would not be present had you just skipped along merrily and got everything you wanted precisely when you wanted it. There would be less appreciation for the journey, and no lessons learned.

Opposition is the force that creates fortitude and stamina and strengthens will. It gets us to answer the question: how much do I really want this? You'll know when you're pursuing your heart's desires when you don't easily give up. You have the staying power to make it through all obstacles because you're powered by the will of your soul and spirit. When you're pursuing things that don't mean much to you on a soul level, you will not have the stamina, endurance, or energy to see these pursuits through to completion when the road gets rough. You'll give up because the pursuit doesn't mean much to you on a soul level and every ounce of your being knows it. Consequently, there's no internal source of power to pull from and your forward momentum is eclipsed.

Opposition is your friend.

There's a beneficial aspect of opposition to keep in mind: just like everything else in universal creation, opposition follows the laws of order and is always proportionate to what our desires and intentions are. The greater the desire and intention, the greater will be the resistance to it and the higher the level of opposition there will be. For your huge dreams and aspirations, you'll have huge obstacles to overcome. For your smaller desires and dreams, the opposition to it will present itself to a lesser degree. All oppositional forces are in direct correlation to the magnitude of our desires and dreams. The desire and its opposition are always equal.

Those who dare to have big "whats" and "whys" are the ones who must overcome the largest of obstacles and who must climb the highest of mountains. Big dreams cost more. There are a multitude of people who sit around and dream big, but few who are willing to pay the high cost those big dreams require.

When it comes to paying the price for your desires, you'll be able to ante up if you have a powerful and compelling reason *why*. Here's how my story relates.

Write or die. That's my *why*. I discovered years ago that I am a writer, designed thus by God. If I didn't write, I'd die. It would be a long, slow, painful death by non-fulfillment, but a death nonetheless. The cost of not being fulfilled on a long-term basis, which is, under the surface, a refusal to grow, causes death. Nature is set up that way. Contribute or die. Be useful, or be used by the cosmos as fertilizer. Either way, you will contribute. I figure it's better to do it voluntarily.

I write every day of my life. My writing intention is supported by a huge *why*: a fulfilled, joyful, and purposeful life. Writing affords me the creative expression of natural gifts and talents from God. Anytime I walk fully in my God-ordained gifts and talents (of which writing is one), I live life more fully, deeply, and richly. I experience deeper levels of gratitude and passion for life that are non-existent when I'm not walking in or living my gift. The feelings that are engendered within me when I write are deeply therapeutic. It's true that I write to be a catalyst for healing, which I pray will happen for those who read what I've written. However, writing these words is, first and foremost, exceptionally healing for me. There's fulfillment in writing for me, whether or not my work is accepted or liked. It makes me feel good to write, and that's what matters most.

What's your *why*? Why do you desire what you desire? As stated earlier, if your whys are weak (in that they don't hold much meaning for you), your will to push forward will not be sufficient to face and overcome the challenges that are inherent in every dream. If you have a powerful why, especially a why that connects to your overall life purpose, you'll be able to face all opposition and challenges with full faith and trust in God's purpose and plan.

What's an example of a weak why? An example of a weak why is desiring more money so you can buy more trinkets or baubles or stuff. Stuff doesn't fulfill, and our soul knows it. When you set out to make more money just to accumulate more stuff, you won't succeed in the long run because part of you knows that more stuff is not tied to any significant purpose, nor is it particularly meaningful for you. If anything, more stuff may actually distract you and keep you from realizing more of your purpose and passions. You may succeed in getting the stuff, and fail in being and feeling fulfilled.

What is an example of a powerful why? An example of a powerful why is desiring more money because you consistently donate 10 percent, 20 percent, or more of your income, and you wish to give away a specific sum of money. For example, let's say your place of worship wants to build or purchase a new building. The desire arises within you to make a contribution, and you'd like it to be beyond anything you've been able to do before. You come up with the idea of gifting a sum of money that you've never gifted before, and it actually thrills you to even think about giving away that much money. If you're a person who contributes 10 percent or more of your income, you know you'll need to generate a lot more money than you have before in order to gift more than you ever have. This desire alone is enough to get forces moving in your direction that support you in making your intention come true, because it is a desire of your heart, and it supports and benefits so many other people. Of course, you'll still need to do the spiritual, emotional, mental, and physical work to bring this goal to physical manifestation. Yet, imagine how excited you'll be in the process, even when things get rough, every time you think of writing a check of that size to an organization you care about.

As you fix in your mind your desire coming true, and you clearly see yourself writing out the huge check, feel the feelings it engenders. Fix that picture firmly in your mind. Intend, pray, and affirm that this desire is now being manifested in your experience.

You'll find that when you run into difficulty attracting the substantial amount of money you desire (which is likely to happen since you've never done this before), you need only keep a vivid picture firmly in mind of the new place of worship. Hold in your mind the scene in which you gift the check to your place of worship. To help you along even further in this endeavor, you can take a check from your checkbook right now and write out the huge check (of course, you won't send it in until you have the money in the bank to cover it!). Take the check and paste it up in a place where you'll see it every day. Don't concern yourself at all with *how* it will happen. Remember, that's a trap: minding God's business is the ultimate downfall. Mind your own business. Your business is internally and externally stating clearly, definitively, specifically, and passionately *what* you desire and *why* you desire it, holding mental pictures of it already fulfilled, feeling the feelings your manifested desire engenders, then taking the inspired action steps to experience your intention and manifest your desire.

As you keep all your mental focus fixed clearly on what you desire and why, allow the great organizing forces of the Universe in the form of synchronicity to work for you. Don't rush the process. Don't be anxious. Relax. After all, when you place an order for flowers, you don't immediately run and fling open your front door, anxiously looking for the delivery man. Instead, you know there exists a period of time during which your order is fulfilled and delivered. In the meantime, you go about your life business as usual. One day, as expected, you come home and find your flowers delivered.

The same is true with all clearly defined desires and intentions. God's love is maximal to the extent that people and resources will come to you without much physical effort or strain on your part. Life is not meant for you to run around working extra hard for your desires to be fulfilled. Life is a lot more fun than that. Probably 90 percent or more of the busy work we do to get what we want is unnecessary or unwarranted. Learn to live by attraction rather than by exertion.

What eliminates the need to work so hard is for you to tune your internal frequency to the God channel. When you're attuned to God's signals, you'll receive all the guidance you require in every millisecond to bring you closer to your life's purpose, passions, and all your heart's desires. We stated earlier the necessity of tapping fully into the voice of God within, in every instance and circumstance. This inner guidance speaks to us in fluid, non-stop bursts of wisdom and awareness that sweep over us continually. It is an internal wellspring of all that is known, including how to fulfill your desires in the most direct and joyful manner, and exists within each of us.

Here's why it's being mentioned again: instead of planning every detail of life, and working so hard at it, there's a pleasant alternative. Stay in full communication at all times with your inner guidance from God. Then you'll know how to proceed in every situation; you'll know where to go and what to do when you get there. This inner knowledge always gives us foolproof guidance; guidance that, if meticulously followed, will provide a cosmic shortcut to all our souls' desires.

Listening to the voice of God takes away the need to plan how everything will turn out. God's voice provides us with the best solutions at each turn for everyone involved.

I'll give you my own story of synchronicity and attunement. I began writing my first book almost ten years before it actually became available for sale. I didn't know anything about the book business when I first started writing; I just knew I wanted to write a book. Since I was a financial advisor at the time, I decided that the book would be about finance and that I would begin it by writing my own story. After I wrote my story, I put the book away. One day, a client who I had not seen in a while came into my office and proceeded to tell me what had transpired in her life over the past few months. She told me that her husband was a heroin addict—unbeknownst to her—and that he was also a convicted bank robber who had spent at least five years in prison. She proceeded to tell me that on their first wedding anniversary, he was short on cash and drugs, so he decided to rob a bank. Her story was so fascinating to me that I felt an instant desire well up within me to write about it. I asked her permission and she agreed. Her story then went into the book. At that point I knew that the book I was writing was no longer a financial book.

I continued working on the manuscript off and on for many years, and added more fascinating true stories to it as I was led to do so. When the yearning to write became too overwhelming for me to continue giving it only back-burner attention, I sold my financial planning practice in order to devote my full time and energies to writing and teaching. Over the next two years I worked on the manuscript, still having no idea how it would get to the marketplace. As I look back on the whole journey, I realize now that I must have had a lot more faith than I thought I did back then. I was completely walking in the dark, or so I thought.

When the manuscript was finished, I decided to go the route of self-publishing. That avenue didn't work for me. Then I decided to go with another author who had self-published many titles and had started a publishing company. That route didn't work either. Then I considered a vanity press. That idea didn't pan out. Then I decided to go with a particular publisher who, I felt, offered what I was looking for. That idea fell apart too. By now, I was seriously wondering how the book would ever get anywhere. All the while, I was praying and attempting to remember that opposition is my friend. At times I felt wobbly, yet I kept going.

One day, I was speaking to a friend of mine (who's also a writer) about writing and I asked him, seemingly out of the clear blue sky, if his agent was accepting any new authors. He told me he would inquire. He got back to me a few days later and told me his agent would look at what I had in the form of a query letter (a short letter used in the publishing industry in which the author tells prospective agents and publishers what the book is about and compelling reasons why they should want to represent or publish it).

I wrote the query letter and sent it to the agent. She was interested in seeing more and requested two chapters of the book. I quickly sent them to her. The agent liked the chapters she read and asked for a book proposal (which is a sales and marketing document all about the book, the market, the author, and why the book will sell like hotcakes). The last time I had written a book proposal had been years before, and I was not happy about having to write one again. Also working as opposition to me was the time frame, since I can be a champion procrastinator. I had to get the proposal done within a tight time frame, as the agent was going to an annual book event where agents and publishers come together with the purpose of selling and buying book ideas. I guess that was God's way of kicking me out of procrastination. Do it now. That was my only option. So I worked on the proposal with the help of the agent.

She and I entered into an agreement for her to sell my work to a publisher. She went to the conference with my book proposal in hand. Within a few months, in October of 2006, I got a call from my agent that I had a two-book deal with a publisher. She informed me that, if I accepted the offer, my first book, *God Speaks to Me*, would be published in November of 2007. I was elated! Almost ten years after I started writing that book, I finally saw *how* it would get to the marketplace. Up until that point, I was working only with *what* I wanted and a very strong *why*. Almost ten years after I had begun writing my first book, in perfect divine order and perfect divine timing, God took care of the *how*.

What I now know is that it doesn't take ten years to write and publish a book, so I am not suggesting that your desires must take a long time. Perhaps my dream of being a published author would have come in different timing had I not been resistant to the process, though I know it all unfolded perfectly for me.

When I look back over the path to publication for my first book, it happened completely by faith in God's creative process. I see clearly how synchronicity played a pivotal role in bringing me into contact with the perfect circumstances, people, situations, and events to have success, even though I had no idea of how it would happen. In the whole process, I simply needed to mind my business by keeping my writing intention firmly in mind, visualizing my desire as already fulfilled, feeling good about it, and consistently and passionately continuing to engage in the activity of quality writing. I stayed open to divine guidance from within and followed it as best I could in each moment. Sometimes I faltered. Sometimes I was hot and on top of my game. Either way, I kept my dream alive. God took care of everything else.

Notice that there were many opportunities for me to give up and not move forward. Door after door slammed shut. Over the years, whenever I tried to market a book idea, I would get nothing but rejection letters. Worse yet, many of them were form rejection letters! I recall Stephen King stating that, in the early days of his writing journey, he received so many rejection letters he could wallpaper a room with them. That thought was one of many that kept me going.

If I had not had a strong *why* that compelled me forward consistently and constantly, I would have given up long ago. And, without knowledge of—and trust in—God's ever-present hand in the creative process, I wouldn't be enjoying the physical manifestation of being a published author, which is both a passionate desire and an essential aspect of my calling as a teacher and creative expressionist.

I hope my story inspires you to mind your business. Let my experience teach you, as it does for me every day, that all you need do is determine clearly what you desire, state why you desire it, picture it clearly and colorfully in mind, feel good about it and then walk by full faith and trust that it will surely be delivered to you, while enthusiastically engaging in inspired action steps that will move you in the direction of your dreams. Have the heart to take the action that your dreams require—and that you're being led to perform in the moment—without fear or hesitation. Step by step, moment by moment, you will be cooperating with (rather than fighting) the great organizing, supernatural force in the Universe called synchronicity. It's God's way of answering the "how" part of the equation.

Remember, God's love is maximal and you are lovingly and automatically granted all your heart's deepest desires. God has one answer to your request to live your highest and best life, the call of your soul; that divine answer is always *yes*. Are you prepared to do what it takes to receive your *yes*?

Thoughts for Today

Today I am relieved to know I don't have to do everything myself.

I celebrate all the seeming coincidences that unfold for me, for they are more evidence of God's maximal love for me in every moment.

As I lovingly consider what I want and create clear and passionate intentions that benefit myself and others, I am richly blessed.

I always get what I expect; therefore, I have the highest and best expectations that honor my God-ordained gifts and talents.

I know God always says Yes, and I do my part so I can receive my Yes.

I am joyful, fulfilled, and vibrantly alive!

Keys

"If you believe, you will receive whatever you
ask for in prayer."
Matthew 21:22 (GNT)

"Your power is so strong that whatever you
believe comes true. You are the way you are
because that is what you believe about yourself.
Your whole reality—everything you believe—is
your creation."
Don Miguel Ruiz, *The Mastery of Love*

Ask in prayer, believe, and receive. Sounds
simple enough, doesn't it?

The question that arises for me with regard to
Jesus' statement is: ***If it is indeed so simple
for us to get what we want, why doesn't
everybody have everything they ask for?***

Quite a number of us still meet with challenge
in following this simple three-step formula for
getting what we want. A large number of this

planet's dwellers don't even have basic necessities, such as clean, clear drinking water and a home to call their own. Surely they've asked. Almost everyone I know has asked.

What's missing? If the formula for fulfillment of desires is to ask (in prayer), believe, and receive, where in this simple three-step process do we get lost? Though this formula appears simple, experience would indicate that it isn't easily implemented. It could take a lifetime to master the immense magic contained within the three keys to the kingdom of ask, believe, receive. Since I'd rather not take a lifetime to learn the secrets to successful implementation (and, I suspect, if you're reading this, perhaps you don't either) let's talk about attaining creative mastery in a much shorter time frame.

The topic of prosperity can be used to explore the implementation of the magical keys to the kingdom, specifically with regard to home ownership. It's a topic of high interest and common desire: to inhabit a haven where we find peace and rest. Most of us have a desire for a place to call home.

I am blessed to have recently purchased a new home. To manifest this dream, I followed the highly simplistic, three-step process Jesus so beautifully outlined: ask in prayer, believe, receive.

Before I talk about the details of using the keys to the kingdom to manifest my dream home, there's something I'd like to explore on a deeper level.

Consciousness creates, and homeownership is yet another example of this dynamic. When we experience a wandering and aimless internal feeling/state of being, a matching external circumstance of homelessness can be created. The condition doesn't always mean that the individual doesn't own a house. There are homeowners who are homeless. Owning a house and having a home are two separate and distinct affairs. Having a home—that is, being at home—is an internal state of being, whereas owning a house is an external condition. One can own a house and still not have a home. Conversely, it is possible to have a home and not own a house. The latter scenario can arise as a result of intentional choice.

I remember a time when my thoughts and feelings were unsettled and restless. It was a period of great unrest in my outer world. One of the outcomes I created was homelessness. I came to know more on this topic than I would have liked. Nevertheless, I learned valuable lessons in the turmoil.

When we don't feel at home within, we're more likely to create a matching external condition of wandering aimlessly from here to there with no place to call home. An inner state characterized by feeling unsettled and separated from the Source of life and love can create—among varied and multiple other unfavorable conditions—a corresponding outer state of homelessness. Not by necessity, but by virtue of the inner state of being. It is never necessary to be homeless, no matter what we tell ourselves; although some of us have created the stressful and undesirable experience to learn valuable lessons.

Let us now return to the magic formula and examine how it helped me focus my energies to attain a new home. The formula works. You've used the formula successfully before, countless times. Yet, I have a feeling you may not have all the desires of your heart. A word of caution is in order here. We will never have all the desires of our heart. As soon as one desire is fulfilled, others arise instantaneously to take their place. The wheel of desire turns endlessly. Therefore, we proceed with caution and wisdom as we create the desires of our heart, always mindful that more desires will continue to crop up like weeds in a garden. As soon as one is plucked, two more grow in its place. This is not to say there is something wrong with desire. It can be looked at in two ways.

First, there are the desires of your heart, your soul's desires. These desires are for joy, passion in living, and total life fulfillment. Being unfulfilled with regard to these desires has been referred to as "divine discontent," which urges us on to fulfill our divine life's purpose. A longing to live on purpose with passion and power and to fulfill our mission here is a desire of the heart. It is your soul's desire to serve and it is insistent. It doesn't go away. Your divine life's purpose doesn't go away. I was created and born to be a teacher and creative expressionist. I fulfill my divine life's purpose by writing, speaking, teaching, and bringing into manifestation creations which express my individuality, talents, gifts, and mission. Your mission can be filled in any way you choose. It is a most worthy desire to fulfill. Each of us has a life purpose that has been impressed upon our mind and heart by God. Each of us is here to do something particular and important. You are vitally important. What you have to offer us is vitally important. Determining what you are here to contribute to the rest of us by way of living your divine life's purpose is a worthy desire to fulfill. It may be one of the only desires worthy of fulfilling.

The desire that burns within—your divine life's purpose seeking your awareness and expression—is a fire that can literally consume you from the inside out. Jeremiah of the Old Testament of the Holy Bible spoke of his calling as a prophet being a burning fire in his bones. He had to speak what God had given him. He referred to his calling and mission as a fire. Jeremiah's words convey the feeling we get when our life's purpose calls out for expression. It is deeply fulfilling to heed the call.

The second class of desires arises from the ego mind, which can never be satisfied. The ego desires things and situations which are temporal and fleeting. The object desired, once obtained, is often despised. An example of this is when one person thinks she truly desires another person sexually. The two parties engage in sexual activity, sometimes only to be disappointed as the desire deteriorates into contempt. The demands and desires of the ego mind are endless: as soon as an ego desire is satiated, another desire emerges, creating an endless and downward spiral of living only to satisfy longings and desires. Such an endless chase keeps us from living on purpose. Trying to satisfy ego desires is vanity.

The kind of desires I am referring to here are the desires of the heart. At times, a desire of the heart may arise in our human mind as a desire for something physical and tangible. For instance, in the desire to have the experience of being secure, and feeling grounded and comfortable, is the human desire for a place called home. A home is not a necessity. We may think it is, but there are millions of homeless people worldwide who are still alive, so it is apparent that a home is not a necessity for living. However, in the Western part of the world where I happen to live as I write this, possessing a home is considered of extreme importance and being homeless is considered an unwanted state. Yet I reiterate: a home is not a necessity for living. I've been homeless and I'm still alive.

To me, a home is a haven. It is a place of peace and rest, a place where comfort, security, safety, and love abound. It is the cradle in which we rock. It is the blanket in which we are swaddled. This is what a home means for me.

When I was homeless, I didn't have feelings of being comforted or comfortable. I didn't feel secure. I didn't feel loved. I didn't feel safe. Because these are the internal feelings I associate with a home, it is little wonder that I created the condition of homelessness.

There is only one effective way to address homelessness, and that is to address the thoughts and feelings which are present. I had to ask myself a hard question: what is happening within me that would lead to the creation of this condition? Getting to the answers was my real work. Discovering why I didn't feel worthy of my own home and why I didn't feel loved enough to have a loving space to call home was my task. Once I found the answers to these questions, and addressed the internal call for love with the application of God's love, my homeless condition corrected itself rather immediately. I thank and praise God that I've never been homeless since.

In the self-discovery process, I came to be able to use the magical keys to the kingdom with greater intention and with more precision. As a result of coming to know that I create my world—every bit of it—I felt empowered to take happy responsibility for my creations. The creations I had concocted that I didn't want (such as homelessness) were replaced with the creations I did want (such as owning and enjoying a new home).

How was I able to use the keys to the kingdom to attain the new home? It all started with a simple yet powerful prayer: *"God, show me your highest and best idea of a home for me and my girls."*

That was it. I said the prayer and I released it to God. This is the first step we're given by Christ: "Ask in prayer."

Though I didn't realize it then, this simple prayer proved to be one of the most liberating acts I could have performed. It granted me freedom from having to figure out what to do. I simply returned to the prayer each time I needed to make a decision about a home. On one occasion the real estate agent took me to see a home for sale in one of the neighborhoods and in the price range I had specified. As soon as I walked in the front door, I asked myself a simple question:

"Is this God's highest and best idea of a home for me and my girls?"

The answer was clearly "no." I told my agent the house was not for me and we turned around and walked out the door.

The next day, my daughter and I went to visit new home communities in a beautiful and blossoming area of Maryland. We saw several fine homes, yet none of them fit perfectly. None of them answered the prayer.

One Sunday evening, I felt the urge to conduct an Internet search for my home. This was unusual for me. I never search the Internet when dealing with real estate. I've always chosen instead to work with experienced real estate professionals. This time, I made an exception. While surfing the Web, I found new home developments in a couple of areas I liked. They were far enough away from the city to have scenic views of nature, yet close enough that we could commute in when we wanted a taste of city life. There was one new home development that intrigued me, since it was in an area surrounded by water. Something in my spirit loves being near the water, so this community really spoke to me. The Web site said there was only one home left in the development. I wondered if the home was still available. It was Sunday evening and the home builder's offices were closed. I would have to wait until Monday morning to inquire about the house.

I called early Monday morning and spoke to a person who represented the builder. She said, "I'm so happy you called. We only have one home left. I think you might like it. It's a stone front . . ."

I didn't hear the rest of her sentence. I didn't have to. When I heard the words "stone front," I froze. I knew, in that very instant, the house was mine. I didn't know the price. I didn't know the address. I didn't know anything about the neighborhood or the neighbors. I didn't need to know any of the details, which, at that point, I considered petty. I knew this house was mine.

The agent kept talking. I missed what she said between the words "stone front" and the time I brought myself back to the conversation. I made an appointment with her to see the house the very next day. I went to bed that night mentally and emotionally celebrating my new home. The fact that I had never seen it had nothing to do with my little celebration.

I got up early the next day, filled with excitement about seeing my new house. I went for my usual morning walk and prayed for the spirit of discernment in all financial matters. When it came time to leave, I hopped in my car and started the ninety-minute drive to my new community. The drive was amazing; picturesque and beautiful, even more spectacular than I had anticipated. The vistas elicited in me deep waves of gratitude for all God's creation.

I reached the development, and as I turned the corner, my eyes landed on my new home. There it stood, as if it had been waiting for me, statuesque and beautiful. Her front was adorned with gorgeous stone in the earth tones and hues I've always loved. Tears came to my eyes. My feelings of certainty deepened: this was definitely my home. I was ready to sign the papers. I didn't need to see anything else, not even the interior.

Before I continue, let me digress and share with you why the home's stone front held such meaning for me. For a long while, I'd had a dream of owning a brand new home. Up until that point,

I'd never lived in a new home before. Every home I'd ever lived in had been inhabited first by other people. Other people had cooked on the stove. Other people had paced the floors. Other people had sat on the toilets.

The thought of having a brand new home of my own was spurred on by the new home developments sprouting up everywhere in my neighborhood. I saw new home after new home being built all around me. None of them were mine. There were two reasons I felt I couldn't have any of them: most were far beyond my price range at the time. In addition, I viewed my financial picture as not being in the best shape to buy a brand new home. Because of these limiting thoughts I chose to hold on to, I didn't believe I would have a new home anytime soon. I had owned several houses before, some of which I had lived in and some of which I had rented out as investment properties. By this time, I'd sold my real estate holdings and was living in a home owned by someone else. For the first time in years, I didn't own a home. Part of me felt homeless, even though I wasn't. I was living in a very beautiful and spacious home.

Then came the decision to separate from my husband. Due to multiple unresolved issues, I knew I needed to be alone. I didn't know what would happen with my relationship, and I didn't care. I just knew I needed to be alone. The desire for a home—and to get it as soon as possible—intensified. Though my dream of owning a new home was still active in the background of my psyche, I didn't care if the home I moved into was new or not. I wanted and needed a home, and I needed it right away. So, because I held the limiting beliefs about my financial picture (not founded upon fact, but upon outdated information) I had mentally decided to rent a place for my girls and me.

I went to the Internet (again, an unusual move for me) and did a search for rental homes in my neighborhood. One Web site featured homes in the area where I wanted to live, and one in particular caught my attention. I excitedly picked up the telephone and immediately dialed the agent's number. I left a message on his voicemail. It was a Friday evening, so I didn't think I would hear back from him right away. When the phone rang a few minutes later, I was surprised when I answered and heard the same voice I'd heard on the voicemail greeting. The agent had called me back. Just that fast. I was already impressed. He and I chatted about what I was looking for and about the property he had listed on the Internet. He shared with me that it was a very nice property and it was in high demand because of its location and price. I told him I wanted to look at it. He asked me why I was considering rental properties rather than purchasing a home. I told him I wasn't ready to purchase a home yet and wanted to move soon. He pressed the issue and added that I should consider purchasing. He suggested that we meet at his office to take a look at my credit reports and overall financial picture.

To even consider what he was suggesting was a huge shift for me. Before this conversation, my mind had been fixated on locating a rental home and quickly moving in. I didn't think I was prepared for the mortgage process, nor did I want to tackle it. My mind was on moving immediately. The agent pushed more. I agreed to meet him so we could review my credit reports, a necessary step whether I would decide to rent a house or buy one.

I went to his office on Saturday morning, the day before seeing my new dream home on the Internet. The agent's demeanor in person matched his phone persona; a good sign. He carried a wide smile and an infectiously cheerful disposition. I liked him immediately. The feeling was solidified when we shook hands and simultaneously, albeit briefly, locked gazes. He led me into a conference room where a long wooden table was encircled by chairs. He motioned for me to sit wherever I chose. I chose to sit at the head of the conference table. Before taking his seat, he asked if I wanted coffee or tea. I opted for tea. While he was out preparing my drink, I sat straight up in my seat, surveying the room and imagining myself as the CEO of a large Fortune 500 corporation. I felt empowered and powerful. My attaché, filled with financial documents, sat upright on the floor beside me. There I was, at the head of the conference room table, armed and ready to prove myself financially viable to the extent that people would hand me their house keys in return for my signature and a check.

After we chatted for a while about the weather and other things people make up to talk about before they handle the business at hand, he informed me that we would be joined by one of his business associates. The associate was a mortgage broker who would pull my credit reports and look over any documentation I had brought with me. If things looked in order, his idea was that I begin the mortgage process. I still wasn't sure I wanted to move forward with purchasing at this point, yet I agreed to have the discussion with the mortgage broker. What did I have to lose?

The mortgage broker pulled my credit reports and gave me the good news. He could definitely get a home loan for me, considering my credit and income. My credit was far better than I had previously thought. I have a skewed way of looking at my financial picture: it's always worse in my mind than it is in reality. This very positive discussion I was having with the mortgage broker about my creditworthiness and financial ability to purchase a home was doing wonders for re-orienting the way I viewed my finances. The shift felt good.

With valuable expertise and input from both the mortgage broker and the real estate agent, I made the decision to move forward with purchasing a home. "No need to throw your money away on a rental when you can buy," the agent urged. His motivation was partly influenced by a sizable commission check looming on the horizon, but I agreed with him. We then discussed how much I would qualify for with regard to home price and monthly mortgage, as well as what I would be comfortable with paying for a home. Once we arrived at numbers that worked for all of us, we were able to proceed with clarity and agreement.

Back to the gorgeous stone front and its meaning for me. For years, elements in the Universe had been moving to bring my strong desires to fulfillment, one way or the other. In particular, two pivotal elements paved the way for manifestation of my dream.

Most mornings out of the week, I'd go for a power walk outdoors. I most frequently walked through the new home developments that were mushrooming all around us. As I walked, I'd smile to myself while imagining that one of the new homes was mine. It became a mental and emotional game for me. I frequently gave thanks while I was outside walking among new homes that belonged to other people. I gave thanks that God was handing out blessings in the form of new houses. It didn't matter who God was handing the blessings out to on that particular day. As long as God was handing out blessings, one day I would receive one. So I happily played my game and continued to give thanks for all the new homes, with no regard for who owned which house.

This was the first element working for me: a powerful desire being fueled by a regular game of imagination that included giving thanks.

At the time, I worked from home. I was—and still am—in the habit of placing pictures and words all about in my environment to remind my conscious mind of what's important. My mind can be easily distracted.

On my desk, under the clear Lucite desk cover, I had placed several pictures which held meaning for me along with inspirational messages. Whenever I sat down at my desk, I would be immediately reminded of what was important. It served to keep my mind on track during the day.

One of the pictures under the clear Lucite desk cover was of a home I thought was absolutely beautiful: a brand new, stone front single family home. I looked at that picture day after day after day.

As I look back and reflect on the scene, something inside me always knew I'd have a house that looked like the one in the picture. I didn't know when it would happen; I just knew it would.

Perhaps now you can understand the reason for the bolt of lightning I felt when the builder's agent said the words "stone front" and why I didn't hear much else after that.

I didn't fully realize it at the time, yet I was in the midst of a powerful creative process that would manifest my new stone front home.

When my eyes first landed on the house, there was an undeniable, unmistakable, affirmative answer to my prayer that seemed to declare, *"Yes! This is God's highest and best idea of a home for me and my girls!"*

I signed the contract for the house the next day, wrote a check for the deposit, and drove away with a quiet knowledge in my heart that all was well.

The first step—to ask in prayer—was undertaken in earnest, as I held that prayer night and day. Shortly after I uttered the prayer, it became a beacon to guide my every step.

Step two: believe. Each time I looked at the picture on my desk, I believed that I'd one day have a house that looked just like the picture. Each time I smiled knowingly at that picture, my belief level rose and never wavered.

Step three: receive. This part can be challenging. After having successfully started the creation process, we can negate our efforts if we don't handle this step with care. If we're not ready, willing, or in a position to, we won't receive God's bountiful blessings. In the unfolding of the manifestation of my home, I opened myself to receive. I took the actions necessary to receive and I prepared my mind, spirit, and body to receive. Receiving may sound easy, yet it can be one of the most difficult steps in the whole process. Most of us would rather give than receive. Doing something nice for someone else can be easier than receiving something nice. It is indeed wonderful to give; it is what we were created to do. However,

I discovered I had to learn how to receive, and receive well. I had to learn to balance the scales. Endless giving, without receiving, can create lack and scarcity. Giving and receiving are the same. To fulfill my desire to become a more generous giver, I had to learn to become a more generous receiver. I had to learn to receive all the blessings God had put my name on, not just a select few. I had to learn that God's hands are bigger than mine, so why not allow my Creator to fill my cup?

Learn to receive with great joy and gladness. Before I learned this lesson, when someone offered to treat me to a meal, I would argue with them. Now, I've learned. I don't argue anymore. When someone says, "I'll take the check," I say, "Thank you!"

With joy and grace we open to God's bounteous blessings by allowing. It is a necessary ingredient in the creative process Jesus outlined: ask in prayer, believe, receive.

My new home is a blessed physical reminder to me of God's love demonstrating itself as supply in action. To be able to co-create with God is our enormous pleasure and our most holy work.

Are you infinitely happy and grateful for the depth of God's love? A love which has provided us with the precise and magical formula to be able to manifest our hearts' desires and to co-create a life of joy and fulfillment?

God is in love with you.

You have the keys to the kingdom.

Thoughts for Today

I am a co-creator with God and I joyfully create a life I love!

I can always change what I see anytime I desire.

I am powerful and exercise dominion and authority over my world.

My outer world can only reflect the state of my inner world.

Today, I pray to maintain peace in my inner world.

I ask in prayer, I believe, and I am an excellent receiver.

I live my life in the beautiful space of knowing my power.

I wield my power lovingly for the benefit of myself and my brothers and sisters.

Choice

"I am now giving you the choice between life
and death, between God's blessing and God's
curse, and I call heaven and earth to witness the
choice you make. Choose life."
Deuteronomy 30:19 (GNT)

"Personal power and authentic self-esteem begin
with the realization that you have a choice about
what to think, what to say, and how to act."
Paul Ferrini, *Love Without Conditions*

You always have choices.

You may not like your choices in a given situation, but that doesn't mean you don't have them.

To state that we have no choices is to affirm that we are victims. This is an untruth, because (as we've already discussed previously) God created each one of us to be a powerful creator—we are made in God's image. God is the Creator of the highest magnitude, and we are junior creators, just like our Parent.

A powerful creator is the exact opposite of a helpless victim.

As powerful creators, we create our world.

Two main modes we use to create our world are our thoughts and our choices. We've already discussed how the power of our most dominant thoughts, intentions, and desires creates our world; now let's see how our choices factor into this equation.

God loved you enough to create you with freedom of choice. You decide exactly what you will participate in and you decide how your life will flow. You decide whether things will be bumpy or smooth, rough or easy, unhappy or happy. It's all your choice. You are the boss of your life. Like any boss, you are called upon to take responsibility when your life goes sour just as readily as you take credit when your life proceeds well. They are two sides of the same coin. If you take responsibility for creating your happiness, you must likewise own the consequences of your poor choices.

This concept can be a difficult one to assimilate. When I first learned it, I resisted. I thought, *If this is true, that I create my life with my thoughts and choices, considering how bad my life is right now,*

I must be some kind of sick puppy to have created this chaos!

Yes, you may feel like I did—if you've created some really sick stuff in your life through poor choices, you may conclude that you must surely be masochistic.

There's good news. Since you created your reality in the first place, you have the power to create something completely new and different. ***You have the power to choose***. Encapsulated in the power to choose is the power to transform your thinking, thereby transforming your reality.

You can change your life today. Just decide and the change will begin.

Yesterday, you may have chosen to smoke. Today, you may decide to make a different choice and breathe free.

Yesterday, you may have chosen to overeat. Today, you may decide that you'll have a salad rather than a bacon cheeseburger with fries and a soda. You may further decide to make other healthy food choices and stick to those choices as a way of life. You may begin to release weight and experience other health benefits. Either way, it's your choice. There are consequences that go along with each choice. When you make a decision, you're agreeing to the collection of consequences that follow, for they flow naturally from your decision.

Yesterday you may have chosen to be physically or verbally abused in a relationship. Today, you may make a different choice based upon the realization of yourself as God's magnificent creation. In so doing, you may decide to leave that relationship, regardless of the losses that may accompany your choice (such as loss of a place to live, or income, or any other possessions). You know God's abundant hand will never fail to supply everything you need even before you need it. Therefore, your life now proceeds differently, in the light of your new and more beneficial *choices*.

These are but a few examples of how our thoughts and choices dictate the course of our lives. When we insist on playing the victim, we believe that there's nothing we can do about our circumstances, that we have no choices. As is stated at the beginning of this chapter, you always have choices. You may not like all your choices, but you do have them.

If you see yourself as the powerful creator you are, you will never again find solace in playing the role of victim in your life.

Remember, God loves you enough to let you decide how to live, thereby allowing you freedom to learn and grow at your own pace. Yet, you are lovingly shown in advance what some of the consequences of your choices may be. Other consequences may come as a total and complete surprise, but every action reproduces according to its kind. So if your initial thought, action, and decision were not beneficial to you, you can surmise that the consequences will not be beneficial to you either.

Conversely, if you make choices that are beneficial to you, you can rest assured that the end result will likely be beneficial to you as well. Even if the end result is not as beneficial as you had expected, your good intentions can cause some situations to turn out for your benefit anyway, even though it may have at first seemed otherwise.

Either way, God's love doesn't diminish for making bad choices, nor can it increase from making good choices. God's love for you is not contingent or dependent upon what choices you make. God's love is always maximal.

Your Creator wants you to be happy and to make wise choices that benefit your life and the lives of others.

God loves you no matter what you decide or choose to do, and thankfully, you always get another opportunity to choose again.

Thoughts for Today

God's love empowers me to make potently positive choices in my life.

I choose to create a joyful, abundant world.

Each day I create my experiences; today I choose to create experiences that uplift, nurture, and benefit myself and all I touch.

I make choices that support my body, mind, and spirit, and that produce health, well-being, prosperity, and happiness.

I am eager to learn the lessons inherent in the results of all my choices.

Whatever I choose today, I rest in the loving arms of God.

Now

"And what I say to you I say to everybody:
Watch (give strict attention, be cautious, active,
and alert)!"
Mark 13:37 (AMP)

"Now is the only point that can take you beyond
the limited confines of the mind."
Eckhart Tolle, *The Power of Now*

My mom used to say that there's no time like the present. She was absolutely right. The most powerful moment ever is the moment you are in right now. There's not a more powerful place to create from than where you are right now. Not where you were yesterday. Not where you hope to be tomorrow.

The present moment is the key to unlocking the mystery to every problem in your life.

Why?

Because there's truly nothing wrong with you at this present moment. It is said that all our problems stem from regret and remorse over the past, or fear and insecurity over the future. If we stopped crying over what happened to us in the past, and stopped fearing what could happen to us in the future, we'd be pretty happy creatures!

I was conducting a coaching session with a couple when I, once again, witnessed this phenomenon. One of the partners was speaking about her hurt and pain over what the other partner had done. In listening closely to her, I became aware of her tendency to habitually return to past situations and, in the process, stir up all the old emotion that was present when the event first occurred. When she was talking about today, she was happy. When she went back to last year, or last month, or even yesterday, and all the sadness it carried for her, she immediately felt terrible. She would instantly sink into emotional despair at the thought of past injuries. When I asked her if she was aware of her tendency to go back to the past, she inquired as to what I meant. I shared with her my observation; each time she went into sad emotional states, it was the result of recounting something undesirable from the past, whether it was how her partner treated her or some other unwanted triggering event. I asked her to continue sharing, while being mindful to stay in the present moment. When she spoke again, she began to tell a story about what had transpired between her and her partner the day before. I interjected with a question, "Is what you are sharing about the past?"

"It just happened yesterday," she replied through tears.

"Is yesterday the past?" I gently pressed.

She thought for a moment and when the realization came over her, she actually chuckled. It was in that precise moment that she became aware of her addiction to past hurts and her habit of falling back into the pain all over again. When she remembered to stay present, she was quite happy.

Now is the only purely perfect moment. There's not one thing wrong with you right now. Being fully present in this current moment is the key to overcoming our negative subconscious conditioning. When we move through life unconsciously, not aware of the present moment, we give our subconscious mind permission to step in and run our lives. We find ourselves repeating negative patterns over and over again. We become tied to our past which automatically creates our future. When we allow our mind to slip regretfully back to the past, or jump anxiously ahead to the future, we are not being fully conscious, aware, and present in the moment. The subconscious mind takes over, getting us through our daily activities. Life runs on auto-pilot and we become robots.

When we awaken to each moment and make conscious decisions about what is best for us in this present moment, we break out of the old, negative conditioning and patterning of the subconscious mind. Life is no longer running on auto-pilot. You are no longer walking mindlessly through life. You wake up to the present moment and live in it fully. You make conscious choices and decisions based on the current moment. Your conscious choices are not steeped in regret over what you didn't do yesterday, nor are they rooted in fear of what will happen tomorrow. Only by being fully present in our daily experiences are we able to consciously choose and decide in each moment what appears to best serve us.

Our subconscious mind is an amazing wonder. It contains the memory of everything that's ever happened to you and it is also the home of everything you believe to be true. The subconscious mind will proceed according to whatever is stored in memory and whatever you believe, good or bad. If your subconscious mind has been programmed for lack (perhaps because your parents raised you in a lack environment) it will continue to reproduce those results whenever you are not present enough to consciously choose something different.

Every human has experienced some level of negative conditioning of the subconscious mind by parents, society, culture, religion, and more.

The messages we've received over the entire course of our lives (including the time we spent in the womb) are all recorded in the perfect computer system we call the subconscious mind. Everything we've learned and have come to believe as true (whether it really is true or not) is stored in the subconscious mind. This immense repository of information is available to us at any and all times. When we are driving to work and our mind is elsewhere, the subconscious mind steps in and takes over. It remembers exactly how to drive a car and it remembers how to get to work. Therefore, you can get in your car, start the ignition, adjust the mirrors and the seat, pull the car out of the driveway or garage, and drive all the way to work without conscious recollection of doing any of it.

The same can happen in life with events that are not as mundane as driving to work. If your subconscious mind has been conditioned for failure in relationships, because you believe you're unworthy or unlovable in some way, or because you saw that played out when you were a child, you'll attract folks who validate your subconscious beliefs. The person you choose as your partner will treat you in an unworthy and unloving way, merely echoing to you what you hold in your belief system. Because you believe this about yourself, you will only attract to yourself others who will believe the same about you, thus proving you right. The only way to get rid of bad relationships is to go within and find the belief system that's causing you to attract these types of negative people and dismantle that belief system. Once the belief that you are unworthy or unloving is dismantled and no longer operating within, you'll not attract people into your life who treat you in an unworthy or unloving fashion. When you love yourself, know your value as a blessed child of God and know yourself as worthy of every good thing, whatever or whoever shows up in your life will reflect that new belief.

The only way to counteract the negative patterning and conditioning of your subconscious mind is to remain aware of, conscious of, and dependent upon God's love to guide you in every situation. It means staying present in each right-now moment.

To break out of the old, negative patterns of the subconscious mind, learn to choose wisely and carefully in the present moment. The only way to do that successfully is to check in with God. You'll see exactly how to do that in the next chapter.

Rushing, urgency, clumsiness, and accidents are all signs of living in the future; thinking about where you need to be next and how fast you can get there. Procrastination, hesitation, and delay are signs of living in the past; thinking about past failures and secretly worrying if the same thing will present itself again.

Learn to be fully present in the right-now moment in your daily living. When you walk down the street, really look at everything around you; notice the small things that your eye doesn't notice when you're rushing past mindlessly. Become deliberate in what you are doing in each moment, giving the task at hand your full attention and care. When you're involved in a project, keep your whole mind and attention on it so as to do your best. Multi-tasking doesn't work for you or for the tasks you're engaged in. It runs counter to staying fully present, as it is not humanly possible to give full presence to multiple things at one time with excellence, deep care, and mindful attention.

I attended an international festival in Washington D.C. not long ago where I saw monks who were visiting from an Eastern country. They were on their hands and knees, fully engaged and engrossed in blowing through tiny straws to move multi-colored sand particles into perfect lines, spheres, and varied other geometric shapes. They were creating a sand mandala. I was intrigued. I'd never seen anything like it before. I stood there mesmerized by their full attention to what seemed to be painstaking detail. I watched them transform multi-colored sand particles into the most intricately beautiful work of art. None of the monks were talking on the cell phone while they were working. None of them were gazing up at the sky. None were chatting with each other. There was only full presence and quiet focus on one endeavor: blowing sand into lines and shapes. It was a reverent and meditative experience for us all.

When you become consciously engaged in each moment, life will be full and rich. You'll notice things you hadn't noticed before. Your senses will be heightened and you'll derive greater pleasure from whatever you choose to engage in. Most importantly, you'll learn to become a conscious creator who makes beneficent choices in the present moment.

Thank you, God, for the wonderful gift of NOW.

Thoughts for Today

This moment is a gift from God for which I am deeply grateful.

I sit in my skin and soak in all the pleasures of this very moment, knowing only this moment is real.

Right now, I make decisions and choices that are beneficial to me.

I am fully present and aware as I consciously create a life I desire.

I decide what is best for me in each moment by connecting with the Infinite Love that dwells at the core of my being.

I am superabundantly blessed right NOW.

And this is so!

Intuition

"Trust in the Lord with all your heart. Never rely on what you think you know."
Proverbs 3:5 (GNT)

"We believe in the direct revelation of truth through our intuitive and spiritual nature. And that anyone may become a revealer of truth . . ."
Ernest Holmes, *The Science of Mind*

You don't need a priest, or a pastor, or a pope, or a shaman, or a visionary, or a seer, or a holy man, or a holy woman to tell you what to do.

You already know what to do.

God's love for you is manifested in an internal guidance system which is capable of helping you with every problem or question you'll ever encounter, and every decision you'll ever face.

It's called intuition.

There's a guiding light inside you that always has the answers to all your questions. Some call it intuition, others call it "inner knowing," and still others call it the "still, small voice within." However you choose to refer to it, intuitive wisdom resides within you, and it is at once a perfect decision-making tool, an early warning system, and a direct channel to Spirit.

I call the system foolproof, meaning that I can't mess it up.

How does intuition work? I think of intuition in terms of a space in each of us that receives messages from God. Let's call it a spiritual e-mail account. Every one of us has this spiritual e-mail account. This particular e-mail account is free and doesn't require any complex mechanical equipment. Messages appear in your in-box instantaneously, any time of the day, regardless of where you're physically located.

God installed the program in you when you were born, to insure a direct link between you and your Creator, and it's operating quite well—messages are flowing in from God to you all day, every day, without fail.

Now here's the kicker: most people don't check their spiritual e-mail.

Therefore, they don't get the messages God is sending.

If that's you, read this sentence carefully: just because you don't perceive God's messages to you doesn't mean they're not being sent. If you check your spiritual e-mail, you may find messages God sent to you decades ago! The messages don't leave, and they're not automatically deleted if you don't check in.

There are three common difficulties we as humans run into with this free spiritual e-mail account from God:

1. Some people don't get the messages because they don't have their computer turned on. If you're not consciously aware of what is going on in your life, and you're operating on auto-pilot most of the time, you're probably out of touch with the spontaneous way God communicates with you. You may have your spiritual computer turned off.

2. Others don't get the messages because they haven't checked their e-mail in years. The computer is turned on: these folks have a measure of spirituality in their lives and are probably devout members of a religion. But they have not made their own conscious choices about how they will live their lives based on their personal internal guidance system. They've been told what to do by others, including priests, pastors, teachers, or parents. These folks have the spiritual com-

puter turned on, but they're not checking their e-mail because they're busy doing exactly what other people tell them to do. Doing exactly what you're told doesn't always lead down a negative path. There are many things to learn on the path to adulthood, so we follow a great deal of what we were told by those who were protecting, rearing, and guiding us.

However, there are areas of your life that would benefit from your conscious, aware choices, based on what God is telling you to do in the moment. You may be surprised at the number of times God's messages for you about the direction you should take may be contrary to what you've been told to do by "authority" figures. When that happens, do you decide to do what you've been doing for most of your life, continuing to listen to the people who tell you what to do, or do you take a stand by following the individualized guidance that was sent especially for you and to you by God?

You get to make your own choices with regard to how to worship and live out your life's purpose based upon your internal knowing of what God is guiding you to do, rather than living your life based upon what you've been told to do by other people. If you're not checking what God wants you to do in each situation, your computer may be turned on, but you're not checking your spiritual e-mail.

3. A third group of folks have the computer turned on, and they check their e-mail regularly and read it thoroughly, but still have difficulty following the guidance presented. I must admit that I have been (and sometimes continue to be) resistant to the "still, small voice within." At times, the message doesn't seem to make logical sense. Other times, the message is prompting me to do or say something which may appear to make me look foolish. Fear sets in. These folks would benefit from an increased faith in God, similar to the gentleman who told Christ that he had faith, but still needed help where he didn't have faith. Faith is called for if we are to make a practice of following through with the guidance we get from God *every time, without exception.*

There are consequences to not following the instructions, guidance, and solutions offered by God at any given time. For example, have you ever had the experience of moving about swiftly, with your mind absent, when a little voice says something helpful to you, like "remember your keys" or "take a different road to work today" or "wear a different pair of shoes today." Not following the helpful hints may have cost you: you may have discovered later that you lost your keys, or the road you normally take to work was backed up for miles with traffic causing you to arrive late, or your brand new suede shoes got ruined when it unexpectedly rained later that day.

One night, I learned a valuable lesson in paying attention to my inner voice of guidance. My husband and I were going to a close friend's surprise fiftieth birthday party. My husband's sister had agreed to watch our youngest daughter that night, so after I'd dropped off our daughter, I came back home to get dressed for the party. When I arrived back home, I got the distinct feeling that we should stay in that night. It was almost as if I heard a voice that said, "stay home." Because I felt obligated to go to my friend's birthday party, I ignored the voice. I got dressed, and though we were late, we left for the party. We stopped on the way at a fast food restaurant because my husband, who was driving, had not eaten anything all afternoon. He wanted something to munch on as we drove to the party. Shortly after leaving the fast food drive-through, my husband, when looking down at his food, ran our car into the back of a van that was stopped at a red light. We hit the van with a loud and explosive bang, and both our airbags popped out, spewing noxious fumes into the air. For a second, I didn't realize what had just occurred. When I came out of my daze, I opened the passenger door of our very crunched vehicle and made my way out. Glass, car fluids, and car parts were strewn all over the street. The car was totaled. Thankfully, both my husband and I were completely unharmed.

As I stood on the side of the road, staring at the wreckage, the words I'd heard earlier came rushing back: "stay home." When I shared my little voice story with my hubby, he stared at me and said, "I got the same message before we left, that we should stay home, but I didn't want to disappoint you by telling you what I was thinking."

Another time this helpful voice is heard is whenever we meet new people. For example, you may have felt an uneasy feeling (for no logical reason) when meeting a new potential romantic partner. You decide to ignore the feeling since this person seems to fit your criteria of a mate and there seems to be no logical reason why you and this person shouldn't be together. You forge ahead in the relationship only to find out later, for whatever reason, this person is the last person you would ever want to be involved with.

Not following the instructions and guidance sent to you via your built-in, spiritual e-mail carries hefty consequences. We always have choices and each choice has a set of consequences attached to it. Just because God sends us a spiritual e-mail obviously doesn't mean we have to follow it. Your guidance doesn't command or demand. There's nothing forcing you to do what God would desire you to do. You always have choices.

Yet if you understand God's one and only desire for you, that your life be filled with love, unbounded joy, limitless happiness, deep fulfillment, true meaning and purpose, harmony, peace, tranquility, and infinite abundance, then you would probably want to follow the guidance you receive.

The following is a three-step process to receiving clear messages from God:

1. Turn your computer on. This means to be *awake and aware* of what is happening in your life and consciously decide to not operate on auto-pilot. Look around and you'll see folks who have pretty much agreed to live in a semicomatose state. They're barely awake: they can get to work, do their job, come home, interact with their family, and go to bed without ever really being actively engaged. They're just going through the motions. They are, in actuality, half asleep.

To have your computer turned on so that you will receive God's e-mail means you are making a choice to come out of your self-induced coma, to become aware of your choices and why you're making them, to become aware of your thoughts (which create your reality), to become aware of the ways you commit self-sabotage, to become aware of what you truly want in your life. In other words, you have to wake up! After you've awakened, you get to decide to live a life of relentless discovery of what's going on in your internal world, so as to be able to clearly see why you do what you do. Only with this awareness can you decide to do something different.

This course and process requires that you become fully aware and awake. When you are aware—as a result of self-discovery—you are more attuned to the voice of Love within.

2. The next step after waking up is to check your spiritual e-mail all day, every day. Learn to check in with your own internal guidance system to determine what's best for you rather than relying on others to tell you what to do. Just because your parents were Baptists, and your grandparents were Baptists, doesn't mean it's your path. Make your own conscious choices and decisions based upon the specialized guidance you're receiving from your loving Creator, moment by moment. This course of action may cause you to break with some habits you've established based upon what other people told you was right for you. I must warn you, it takes an immense amount of courage to break with the customs that have been handed down to us so that we may walk our own authentic paths. Yet this is the path of greatest fulfillment. God is not concerned with you following customs and traditions that have existed in your family, culture, and/or religion for years if following those customs is not authentically you. God is concerned with you having the faith to walk your own path, the path prepared expressly for you before you were born and the path that brings the greatest gladness to your heart. Only you can walk your path. You may discover that your unique path melds or merges with your parents', or you may find yourself striking out into completely virgin territory. Either way, God's got your back.

3. The third step in the process is following the guidance provided. Each of us has received messages from God that we didn't follow and later regretted it. The reason we usually ignore, argue with, or simply dismiss most of the messages we get from God is because they don't seem to make logical sense, or they call on us to do scary or unusual things. The mere thought of doing what God is guiding us to do has the power to absolutely terrify. Multiple fears can arise:

If I go for it and fail, I'll look foolish. If I do (fill in the blank), what will people think of me? If I say (fill in the blank), what will people think of me? I've never done that before; I wouldn't even know how to begin. I don't have enough money to do that. I can't move to that part of the country; I don't know anyone there. I would love to start the business of my dreams, but now is just not the right time.

These are just a few of the excuses we use to placate ourselves about not following our internal guidance system and its urges to be better and to live better. When we're not following the messages that are being continually sent to our spiritual e-mail account, we're missing out on life's best possibilities.

An example of this was observed in a young lady who attended one of my retreats. She's quite intelligent, successful, and attractive, with lots of positive things in her life. However, she had a continual inner urge to leave her job to pursue her passion. She had actually reached the point where she deeply disliked going to work. When I asked her what stopped her from leaving her job and doing what she really wanted to do, she replied, "I won't have a job."

"And what's wrong with that? You don't want the job you have anyway," I pointed out.

"If I don't have a job, I'll become homeless." She was making quite a leap here, to jump (in her thinking) from leaving her job to becoming homeless. It certainly isn't a given that if you don't have a job you'll automatically become homeless.

My response was, "Squirrels are homeless, deer are homeless, birds are homeless, and they're doing perfectly fine."

Having been homeless for a spell myself years earlier, I knew homelessness could turn out to be just another dip in life's road. I was not advocating homelessness. I was pointing to a simple truth: when we're internally guided to take a particular course of action, Love is guiding us, and all the provisions for the path have already been made. God never asks us to do anything without giving us everything we need—internally and externally—to be fully prepared to handle all we'll encounter.

From our tiny, human vantage point, we may not see all the provisions that have already been placed on the path for us. The path twists and turns; it's not laid out in a straight line. We're not able to see everything in advance. That's why it's called faith—believing in something we don't currently see.

God may be urging you to do something right now, but you may lack the faith to strike out boldly and do it. If that's your current situation, as it is with so many people I meet, it would be beneficial for you to build your faith. Life becomes nothing short of magical when you develop the faith and courage to follow God's guidance to you in every situation, throughout each day. Following God's guidance within is like giving yourself a magic wand: things will start to turn out exactly as you would like them to. This is because there's built-in help and resources along the path God has paved for you. When you take the high road God leads you on, you'll meet the right people at the right time. You'll travel farther, faster. You'll get all sorts of help from people and they may not even know why

they're helping you. You'll see things start to go
your way for no apparent reason. When you go
in the direction God is pointing you, all kinds of
good things will come your way, and they'll come
easily. You'll live what people call a charmed life.
People will look at you and say, "That person is
undeniably blessed! I wish I could be like that!"

What they don't realize is that we *all* can live
a life like that, because we *all* have the internal
guidance system that has the power to radically
transform our lives. We need only pray for the
faith and courage to follow the guidance as it is
provided.

Realize that your intuition (or your spiritual
e-mail) can show up for you in any number of
ways:

Physical sensations: which may include
chills, tingling, cold hands or feet, heat and/or
perspiration, hairs on your body standing up.
Always listen to your body. It tells you everything you need to know. When things aren't right
around you, your body will tell you.

Strong Emotions: whenever strong emotions arise in us, we want to pay close attention. Crying, sadness, fear, anger, jealousy, and
all other emotions, either positive or negative,
serve as signals. These emotions could be triggered by our own internal unresolved issues that

are made to manifest when a certain person is around us, or the strong emotion may be telling us not to proceed. Whatever the strong emotion is that you are feeling, pay close attention. Sit silently and ask what it means. Then proceed consciously and mindfully.

Instant Knowing: this is one of the ways my personal guidance system speaks to me. I will suddenly and instantly know information that is valuable to me or someone around me. The information provided is not derived from any of the five senses. Instant knowing is spontaneous and arises as a certainty, not a question. Usually, the more you think about instant knowing, the less intuitive it becomes. The power of instant knowing is that it arises spontaneously from a place deep within you, not from your conscious, thinking mind. Often, you're not able to explain how you know something, you just instantly know it.

Hearing Voices: some of us hear voices. Though this may sound crazy to some, it isn't crazy when the source of the voices is God within. It's up to you to determine where the voices originate. This is a learning process which may take years. Eventually, you'll recognize the ring of truth that accompanies hearing God's voice of wisdom within.

Seeing Mental Images: sometimes a picture or an image may pop into our heads that has significance. Somewhere deep inside, we usually know what the image or picture means, and how it relates to our experience.

Memories: sometimes a memory will flash into our heads of a prior success or other good experience we've had, which will show us how to proceed in the present moment.

There are an unlimited number of ways we could receive spiritual guidance via our intuition. God is not limited in communing with you. It is a very personal matter and varies with each of us. However God speaks to you, learn to listen and develop the faith to follow through.

Before I conclude this chapter, let me make mention of the exact opposite of receiving messages from God internally, and that is the feeling that we have no guidance from God or don't know what to do.

For those times when you're seeking guidance and haven't received a clear answer, the following story may help you. It goes like this:

Buddha, accompanied by some of his disciples, was traveling across dusty roads, and suddenly became thirsty. Ananda was one of Buddha's disciples who had decided to follow him, and had volunteered to serve Buddha's corporeal needs. Buddha gave Ananda his wooden bowl and asked him to walk back about two to three miles to a river they had passed, to fetch him a drink of cold water. Ananda made the two to three mile walk back to the river. When he arrived at the river's edge, a horse and wagon had just crossed the river, dredging up dirt from the river's bed. When Ananda put Buddha's wooden bowl in the river, the water he drew was full of silt and dirt. So Ananda walked back to Buddha and told him what had transpired. Buddha told Ananda to go back to the river, and please fetch him some cold, clear water. Ananda turned and began the walk back to the river. When he arrived at the river's edge for the second time and dipped the bowl in, he saw that the amount of silt and dirt in the water had diminished, but had not entirely disappeared. It was then that Ananda got the internal revelation to sit by the river's edge until the water was perfectly clear, before again attempting to draw water. It was in that moment that Ananda learned a most important spiritual principle: wait for clarity. Ananda sat by the water's edge for quite some time, until all the dirt settled back down to the river bed. When the river was clear and settled, Ananda dipped the bowl into the river and drew from it a refreshing bowl of clear water.

When you require guidance, and you think you don't hear God's voice, or you don't hear it as clearly as you'd like, wait for clarity. Sit in the stillness and do nothing. Clear the river of your mind. Allow your thoughts to settle. Sit in the quiet serenity of your settled, surrendered mind. Wait for clarity and it will surely come.

God's love provides you with help in making all your decisions, and thankfully, the guidance is always foolproof.

Thoughts for Today

God loves me and I am gifted with an internal guidance system, which is fail-safe and foolproof.

The clearer and cleaner I keep my internal system—by keeping my mind and heart free—the better I am able to hear and respond to God's voice.

*God guides me—I always know what to do.
As God speaks, I listen and act in accord with divine guidance.
Today, I practice listening to my internal wisdom from God.*

I am grateful for the messages I receive from Spirit.

*Today, this is my prayer:
I am divine.
I always know what to do.
God is now showing me the way.
I am joyful. I am happy.
I am thankful.
Amen.*

Prayer

"Do all this in prayer, asking for God's help.
Pray on every occasion, as the Spirit leads."
Ephesians 6:18 (GNT)

"The person who prays daily is certain to succeed,
because he is attuning himself to the richest, most
successful force in the universe."
Catherine Ponder, *The Dynamic Laws of Prosperity*

We have a direct line of communication with the Creator: it is called prayer. The line is never busy. Caller ID is not necessary; your call is always welcomed. There's no call waiting; the Creator can handle several calls at the same time. There's no call blocking; God always accepts your calls.

The line is never out of service. It's open to you every day, all day. You have a direct channel to God.

Prayer has a different connotation for each of us, based on our life experiences and our relationship with the Creator. Some have an ambivalent attitude toward God, while some are angry at God. They feel God took someone away from them prematurely, or they feel their calls for help went unanswered. Some feel God let something terrible happen to them that never should have happened.

Whatever your feelings about God, there is but one answer: ***pray***.

Pray if you hate God. Pray if you're angry with God. Pray if you think God let things happen that should not have. *No matter what, pray, and keep on praying until something happens in you, to you, or for you.*

Prayer is the solution to every question.

When we pray, we're taking time to turn our conscious awareness and focus to the Creator of all that is. We raise our attention to a level higher than any problem, which elevates our view. From an elevated view, we're able to see more and to see more clearly, just as one is able to see from a higher and more expanded vantage point when standing on top of a mountain than when standing on low ground. An elevated view, by its very nature, is more all-encompassing than a close-up view. When we pray, we effectively take our eyes off the problem at hand and turn our eyes to God, whose thoughts are loftier than ours. From this higher elevation, it becomes apparent to us that all things are possible with God. It's difficult to remember how omniscient, omnipotent, and omnipresent God is when our focus is fixed on problems. Yet, when we take but a moment in earnest, sincere, and heartfelt prayer, we begin to fix our focus on the infinite nature of the living God, which demonstrates for us, in every instance, that the answers are already present. We simply want to become aware of them.

God is in love with you, so you are assured an answer. The answers may not appear when you think they should, yet they come in perfect time; God's perfect time.

As you pray in the midst of your difficulties, the haze that obscures your vision lifts, and you're able to clearly ascertain the beauty of each moment and its inherent perfection. You are, right in the midst of difficulty, learning the most valuable lessons, which, once mastered, propel you to new heights. Prayer is the tool to keep you present to the inherent beauty that is ever unfolding beneath your troubles. Prayer keeps you anchored to the truth.

Before presenting ourselves in prayer to our Almighty Creator, appropriate preparation is in order. We prepare ourselves before engaging in any activity that holds deep import for us; likewise with our prayer practice. Here are useful ideas to consider as you prepare to pray:

1. Go to a quiet place—preferably the same quiet place. Have a space designated in your home for prayer. If you don't already have one, create the space now. In ancient times, the high priests offered prayers in the temple, a dedicated place for worship. In modern times, an altar appears in most holy places, which symbolizes communion with the Divine. Devoting a space in your home to the practice of prayer speaks to all levels of your mind and body, and serves as a gentle encouragement and reminder—in the natural—to pray without ceasing. It makes a statement to the Universe that you are dedicating and consecrating a space to what you hold as vitally important. What could be more important than your spiritual practice?

Your sacred place can be a cozy corner or a sprawling space. Size doesn't matter; whether you live in a jail cell, a hut, or a mansion, you can designate a space for prayer. The focus here is on bringing a higher level of spiritual energy into your dwelling. You are energizing your space with the holiness of prayer. Soon, your space will take on its own sacred energy, which flows from your personal prayer practice. Your space will become imbued with reverence; a reverence that emerges in spaces where consecrated worship and prayer happen often.

You may feel led to place items in your prayer space that hold deep spiritual significance to you, such as a cross, an angel, or butterflies. What you add is a matter of personal preference and is solely for you. You are the gatekeeper of your mind, so what you add to this space should represent a sacred connection to your Creator. Only you know what that means to you. This varies with each person.

In my prayer room, affectionately called Heavenly Splendor, in addition to the seat I use for dedicated times of prayer and meditation (with its own pillows and prayer blankets), there are spiritual texts and books, my journals, pictures and statues of angels, an altar, and other symbols of spiritual significance to me.

Creating your sacred space can be one of the most powerful ways to shift your thoughts and feelings to a higher level.

Be bold and create this space in your office, or place of work, too. An altar in your workplace can be powerful for shifting the energy of the entire office. One of my favorite guidelines in life is: it's better to ask forgiveness than to ask permis-

sion. With that said, you might not want to go to
your boss or the person you report to and ask if
it's okay to build an altar in the office.

Instead, simply clear a space in your work area
and add an item to it that's non-offensive and
perhaps may not even be noticeable to the people
you work with. It could be a white candle (which
you don't light—to be safe), or a picture of a wa-
terfall, or a nature setting. Your workplace sacred
area doesn't have to look like a religious edifice.
You are simply placing in your office a symbol
which reminds you to stay in communion with
the Divine.

Whatever your sacred space looks like or wherever it is located, may it be a space that uplifts you
in prayer and Holy Communion.

1. **Take several deep breaths before beginning to pray.** Deep breathing clears
   the body of toxins. It is said that 70 percent
   of the body's toxins are released through the
   breath. We've heard of "clearing the air."
   Deep breathing clears the spiritual air within us and around us as we prepare to pray.
   As you breathe deeply, draw your shoulders
   back and feel your chest expand. Slowly in-
   hale the air deep into your abdomen. As you
   exhale slowly, relax and physically release
   all tension.

2. **Release wandering thoughts by clearing your mind.** Deep breathing aids you in the process of releasing mental and emotional baggage before you pray. Think of it as entering your prayer room after you've dropped all your heavy bags at the door. You are preparing your mind and heart to speak to the Creator. Clear your mind of clutter, and conflicting and negative thoughts, and turn your attention inward to your heart where you touch the Source of all supply. All such negative energies inhibit prayer, so take the time now, before praying, to silence your mental noise. Remember: "be still and know ye are God."

By creating and consecrating a sacred space, by breathing deeply and calming your mind and heart, you have well prepared yourself to engage in the most powerful communion ever: communion with your loving Creator.

Of course, there are times when we may be in an urgent situation, and there is not sufficient time for lengthy preparation before uttering a prayer. There are occasions that warrant a quickly uttered prayer. However, if our prayer practice only and always features prayers that are uttered in urgency, it would behoove us to ask if we're praying proactively, when no urgency exists.

You may find that the more proactive prayer practice you create and engage in, the less urgent prayers you'll utter.

A proactive prayer practice can be started simply by getting up early in the morning to communicate earnestly with God before beginning your day. People all over the world have found the early morning hours to be a powerful time for prayer, and awaken just before the sun rises in order to more deeply connect with God. (I recently began a practice of prayer, meditation, and devotion from 4:00 A.M. to 6:00 A.M. each morning and it has become a powerful process for spiritual growth and radical transformation.) Again, the more proactive prayers we offer, the less urgent all our prayers become.

A proactive prayer practice includes more than morning prayers. It includes offering prayer throughout the day, which reminds us and gives us opportunity to lift our consciousness all day, every day. Each time we pray, we lift our minds and hearts to God. Each time we lift our minds and hearts to God, we step more fully into alignment with God's perfect plan for our lives. God could just reach down here and do everything for us, but we would quickly bore of life without the push to grow. Life seeks expression and expansion. Your life seeks expression and expansion. Because expansion tends to knock you out of your comfort zone, it can be, at times, uncomfortable, yet it is a prerequisite for a desirable outcome: a joyful, fulfilled, abundant, and purposeful life.

Prayer brings you back home, to the remembrance of the omnipotence, omnipresence, and omniscience of the Creator.

There are several kinds of prayer, including:

1. Thank you, God! This is a prayer of thanksgiving for all God has abundantly supplied to you and for you. To get you started on the road to continual praise, ask yourself: am I alive? This is reason to be deeply grateful. As long as you are alive, you can keep growing, keep working toward all you desire, and keep learning from your choices. You can get to work addressing whatever you'd like to change in your life, no matter how horrific it may appear to be. As long as you are alive, you have reason to praise.

Thank God for the breath in your body, even if your body doesn't work as perfectly as it was originally designed to do. Offer prayers of thanks even if you're lying in a sickbed and can't get up just yet. Offer prayers of thanks if you're not able to walk right now. Offer thanks if you're near death's door. Pray for the Angel of Death to escort you gently and peacefully to the other side, or pray for the Angel of Death to come back much later. Pray and give God thanks.

2. I need your help, God! This prayer may be an urgent one, as in the case of walking down the street and feeling unsafe, or it could be a call for other types of help, such as wanting guidance about what to do in a particularly trying circumstance. Whatever help you need, it's available to you. Just ask. In most cases, help is on the way before you ask. Ask anyway. When you ask, keep one thing in mind: release your specifications for how God should provide help. Some of us are so busy giving God a laundry list of our expectations that we leave no room for God to bring us an even better result than we could've known to ask for.

Help from God could take any form, or it could come from a source or person you never thought would help. Be open to the help, however it shows up. Reverend Jim Webb at the church I attend has a great saying: "God is able to use an infinite number of people to bless you in an infinite number of ways." Don't tie God's hands in your mind. God is in love with you and has already provided what you need, before you knew you needed it. Your job is to be open to receiving it, in whatever form it may appear. You may be surprised at who comes to your aid. You may be sent a helper who is of a different race or religion; a race or religion that you may have had negative connotations about. This could be God's way of getting you to drop some of your limited and limiting beliefs. When praying for help, remain open.

3. God, I want to have the Christ mind. Show me how. This prayer is powerfully transformative. You're asking for guidance on how you can transform your consciousness, which will most assuredly transform your entire life. When you pray for and develop the Christ consciousness, everything else imaginable falls into perfect order and harmony.

On occasion, we may wonder why our prayers seem to go unanswered. The reason some prayers seem to go unanswered is not because God is not listening, nor is it because God has categorically denied the request. God can only grant us what we are willing to accept. In order for us to have the experiences for which we are continually praying, we must evolve into the person who receives and lives these experiences. Jesus said that it is unwise to pour new wine into old wineskins. New wine expands, which would rupture old wineskins, causing the wine to be lost. The same is true of your consciousness. In your present state of consciousness, you may not be able to handle what you're asking for. God doesn't pour new wine into old wineskins. Our loving Creator knows what each of us can handle in the current state of our being. Our consciousness molds and shapes what we receive as an answer to our prayers. To receive more, we must first develop our consciousness to the point where we can receive and hold what we're praying for. It isn't wise to pray for something and expect it to just show up, with God doing all the work. When you pray, be willing to take inspired action in harmony with the prayer, and be willing to develop your consciousness to higher levels that can sustain the answers to your prayers.

Let's use an example of what seems to be a common prayer: praying for more money. I'll use an amount I hear frequently when I teach financial workshops: a million dollars. This seems to be a magical number in many people's minds with regard to financial success. Becoming a millionaire is a goal and pursuit of many folks, including myself at one point.

You find yourself in lack, and desirous of the ability to dream and think big. So you begin to consistently pray for a more prosperous mindset and for a million dollars, which is something you've never done before. A year goes by, or two, and not one extra dollar has shown up on your doorstep, let alone a million dollars. You're no closer to a million dollars than you were when you first started.

Does this mean your prayer is unanswered? No. What it means is simply this: you can pray to God for a prosperity mindset and a million dollars all you want, but if you haven't done the internal work to build a prosperity mindset, and if you haven't developed the consciousness to attract and steward a million dollars, nor have you taken the inspired external action to attain the million dollars, that prayer will seem to go unanswered. It's not that God is withholding the million dollars from you; you're not yet the person who could attract and be a wise steward of a million dollars. Therefore, it doesn't happen. The million dollars does exist, because, in God's world, there is only abundance, and God certainly has more than a million dollars. Further, God has nothing against giving you a million dollars, or more, if that's what you truly desire for purposes of enhancing lives. The question becomes: God has made a million dollars available to you, but are you available to it?

Think of this principle in terms of an electrical outlet and a lamp. Electricity is always available in the electrical outlet. Yet, if you don't plug the lamp in, it will never turn on. You can stand next to the empty socket all day, praying, begging, and pleading for the lamp to light up, with no result. The same is true of a prayer for increased abundance. Abundance is like electricity: always available. Once again, the question is: are you plugged in?

Prayer works in harmony with universal law. The Law of Mind informs us that all things are created by intelligence, or mind. Your world and experiences are created within the realm of thought. The Law of Correspondence states: "as above, so below." We pray, in the Lord's prayer, for God's will to be done on earth (in the natural world of physicality) as it is in heaven (the invisible realm of thought and spirit). A joy-filled, purposeful, and abundantly prosperous life spontaneously bursts forth from a joy-filled, purposeful, abundantly prosperous consciousness. This is the Christ consciousness: the consciousness of oneness with our Creator and all that is. Remembering our oneness with our all-providing Source means we never lack for anything good. We already have everything we need. As a child of God, it's impossible for you to be impoverished, regardless of what you've told yourself. Praying for the Christ consciousness is a prayer for healing all thoughts in your mind which lead to anything other than a supernaturally blessed life.

This is not to say that your life would never have any problems or challenges. Challenges, conflict, and resistance exist to make us better, sharper, and stronger.

However, the Christ consciousness enables us to live in more fulfilling and joyful ways than any life we would have ever been able to achieve without it, while simultaneously empowering us to meet any challenge, conflict, or resistance with a level of faith that would make failure impossible. With God, all things are possible (Matthew 19:26).

Praying for the Christ consciousness is a prayer for faith, endurance, joy, peace, fulfillment, enlightenment, kindness, compassion, and every other Christlike quality. This prayer is always and immediately answered.

4. Prayers for supplication. This prayer is a request to God for what we desire, while knowing it already exists; we simply have to align ourselves with it. Be mindful, once again, of your willingness to do the work (internal and external) associated with being able to attract and handle what you're praying for. Be mindful of what you are asking for and of your capacity to handle, with excellence and wisdom, whatever you are requesting. Our prayers are always answered, even though we may not always recognize the answer.

Prayers for supplication may be offered as an affirmation, which is a statement of fact, or as a request. For instance, if we're praying for more faith, we affirm faith is ours now, as there is no reason that God would not want us to have more faith now. Or, we can simply ask for more faith. I love what the man in the Bible account told Jesus: he stated that he had faith, but he also asked for help where he needed more faith. This man symbolizes most of us, I believe, as many of us have some level of faith, but desire to build more faith. We need God's holy spirit to fill the empty spaces where we feel we are lacking faith.

5. Prayers for others. Intercessory prayers are offered on behalf of others. All of us have a direct line of communication to our Creator, yet we benefit immensely from the prayers of others. It is at these times that those who love us can "stand in the gap," praying on our behalf. At other times, we offer prayers on behalf of those we love, or those we know who may be facing a challenge.

When we offer intercessory prayers, our prayer is not necessarily for the person to be rid of whatever seems to be ailing them. Our prayer is most powerful if we offer it with the knowledge and conviction that all things work together for good. All things. We may, in our human perception, view another's pain and determine they are suffering greatly or unduly. We don't know what uniquely valuable lessons they will learn from their challenge, nor is it up to us to judge their situation. Many a spiritual breakthrough has come on the heels of what looks like extreme pain and suffering. To you, someone else's pain may seem unbearable, though it is precisely what is needed for that soul to learn the vital lessons present. The same is true when others may look at you and wonder how you can bear whatever you are carrying. Onlookers do not know the minds of those involved, nor do they know the broader outworking of God's perfect will.

Our loving Creator knows what each of us can bear, and will never allow us to experience anything that would completely destroy us. So our view of pain becomes one in which we look for the lesson present, while holding firmly to the conviction that all things work together for our good. We remain in the awareness that God knows what is best for all involved, and is working everything out perfectly, in perfect time. Thus, we pray for the best outcome for all involved, not for the solution we think is best. Our interpretation of events is generally flawed, and our view of situations is blind when we consider what God sees and knows. When we pray for others, we leave the solutions to God by asking God to solve the issue in the highest and best way for all involved. We pray for the person to become aware of the answers—which are already present—and learn the lessons quickly and readily so they will ascend to higher ground. There is a reason for every so-called "problem." Our job is to swiftly learn what it's here to teach us and move on. Intercessory prayers support us in doing that.

We offer intercessory prayers for leaders who have positions of great responsibility, including world rulers, pastors, and others who minister to spiritual needs of the flock, leaders in the world of business, and teachers. Reminiscent of Solomon's request, our prayer for leaders is that they be endowed with wisdom from on high.

God loves us so; we each have a direct line of communication to our Source that is always open and available. Pray without ceasing.

God is in love with you. To have a premiere experience of God's love, plunge yourself deeply, fervently, and reverently into prayer as often as you breathe. Allow your life to become a prayer.

Thoughts for Today

God loves me so—I have a direct line of communication to my Creator.

Today I pray with a deep and profound awareness of my ever-present connection to the Source of all life and abundance.

My sacred space reminds me to stay connected to the Divine.

Prayer brings me back home.

I am lifted when I pray for others.

My consciousness is flooded with Light, which enlivens my prayers.

I pray and I take inspired action.

I pray and I feel good.

I allow my life to become an uninterrupted prayer.

Amen.

Meditation

"But his delight and desire are in the law of the
Lord, and on His law (the precepts, the
instructions, the teachings of God) he
habitually meditates . . ."
Psalms 1:2 (AMP)

"Spiritual meditation is the pathway to Divinity."
James Allen, *The Way of Peace*

Prayer is talking to God.

Meditation is listening to God.

I clearly remember the first time I attempted
meditation. I had been told to quiet my mind.
The trouble was I didn't know how to quiet my
mind any more than I knew how to fly to the
moon. I tried to quiet my thoughts. I tried not to
think about anything. I tried to be quiet enough to
hear the still, small voice within that people kept
talking about. It didn't work. The whole episode
ended when my mind pulled a major mutiny.

In the session, I came face to face with the part of me that didn't want to meditate; the internal influence that absolutely insisted on being noisy, and fiercely resisted any attempts at quiet. I named this influence the "mind chatterer."

The mind chatterer launched a mental onslaught every time I tried to get quiet. Each time I sat down to attempt meditation, in would rush thoughts about the laundry, what was in the fridge to eat, what the kids were going to do that day, where I had to go later, what I was going to wear, and how I was going to get there. Random thoughts linked together in an endless stream paraded through my mind. The more I tried to resist, the louder the mind chatterer became. It asked me what I thought I was doing. The chatterer frequently announced that this meditation thing would never work. She called the whole thing crazy and naïve. *What's the point of this anyway?*

All these thoughts and more would occur to me during the first eight seconds or so of my meditation. You can imagine what the next few minutes were like.

As you can see, my first few appointments to get quiet and listen to God didn't work out according to plan.

Thankfully, God is so much in love with me that I was led to teachers who instructed me patiently and lovingly on how to quiet myself long enough to be present to the Presence.

I'm happy to state that my meditation practice has improved, and I'm richer for it. I'm able to reach the point of communion with the inner wise one. I enjoy inner stillness and tranquility. There are still moments when the mind chatterer decides to add a comment or two here and there. I thank her, bless the thought, and release it. As a result, daily meditation has become a practice and a discipline that's enriched my inner and outer worlds beyond description. Its power is second only to prayer and praise. The inner peace, tranquility, and harmony that grow out of a regular meditation practice are well worth the time and effort required to calm the mind and quiet the spirit.

Besides being good for your health, there are distinct mental, emotional, and spiritual benefits derived from a regular meditative practice:

- The peace and stillness experienced during meditation spill over into everyday life. When we're faced with potentially unpleasant situations and people, the inner harmony remembered during meditation brings peace to all of life's affairs.

- Our inner peace is reflected in the outer world. Our external state of affairs—which is now present as the circumstances and conditions of life—was created by our internal state of affairs. Meditation allows us to re-create the inner world where thoughts and feelings reside, which automatically re-creates the outer world of conditions that manifest as our life experience.

- Meditation strengthens our discernment. All of us have a mind chatterer, maybe even several. A number of internal voices speak at once. They can be loud and obnoxious. With so many internal voices, how do we determine which ones are helpful and which ones aren't? Meditation allows us to clearly discern which voices are for us and which are not. The ability to detect, identify, and manage internal voices is radically transformative.

- Meditation begets forgiveness. As we sit in silence, it becomes apparent to us what is truly important. Many of the things we have not forgiven are not important and have nothing to do with our life today. Meditation softens the mind, thus allowing it to more easily let go of old pain.

- Meditation teaches us to be kind by moving slower. I used to rush. I'm still working on releasing the need to walk fast everywhere I go. It was easy to blame my behavior on the excuse I had relied on for years: I'm from New York; we have to move fast. Meditation taught me to slow down and pay attention. When I did, I was able to become a kinder person. Taking the time to be kind to everyone we meet creates such a powerful flow of blessings toward us that it becomes impossible to be unfulfilled.

- Meditation bolsters internal strength and fortitude. It's been my experience that the practice of quieting my mind on demand has developed a discipline within that engenders new levels of mental and emotional strength and fortitude. I started out with baby steps: I would say the word "suspend" to myself, which was my signal to suspend all thought for as long as I could. At first, it was almost impossible to suspend mental busyness. I persisted. As time went on, I could quiet my mind for a few seconds, then a precious couple of minutes, and so on. It was—and continues to be—a gradual process of growth and discovery.

- Meditation instills sanity in a seemingly stress-filled and insane world. I am startled by the climbing volume of people who take pills for stress disorders. There are pills for every known mental and emotional condition. The corresponding commercials urge, "ask your doctor if this pill is right for you" after the fear has been subliminally planted that we have all the symptoms and definitely need that pill. The need for medications may naturally fall away once the mind has been trained for positive reflection upon the goodness of God and our inherent oneness with that good. This is not a recommendation to stop taking prescription drugs. It is a recommendation and an invitation to give yourself the gift of quiet solitude where you place yourself fully in God's hands and feel the depth, breadth, and richness of God's unconditional love for you. No drug could even come close to that experience.

- Meditation dissolves fear and reminds us of the truth: all is well and there is nothing to fear. When we are quiet enough to return to the spirit within that has never been afraid, fear dissolves spontaneously.

- Meditation teaches us to love ourselves, eliminating the drive to look for love in all the wrong places. There's only one Source from which all love emanates: God. When you know this, you will never again be reliant or dependent upon love from someone else. While it's true that giving and receiving love adds a sweet and delectable joy to life, before we can fully give or receive love in all its magnificent aspects, we must first experience and live in the fullness of God's love. Meditative moments of quiet and sweet surrender plunge us headlong into the ocean of God's love. God's unconditional love gives rise to higher levels of self-love. Reflecting on the fullness of God's unconditional love for us is enough to remind us of how truly lovable we each are, in our own peculiar way. When you come to see yourself as fully and unconditionally lovable, you will no longer tolerate or allow unloving behavior of any kind, in any form, from anyone.

- Meditation teaches us to love others. During quiet moments, we come to this truth: everyone is only doing the best they can at any given moment. When we know better, we do better. Waking up to this truth allows us to let everyone off the hook for everything.

- Meditation raises your vibration. All of us are made of atoms and molecules which are in continual movement. We each vibrate at a certain frequency. We are each sending out specific signals. We attract people whose signal matches a signal we are emitting. We attract any and everything that carries a vibration similar to our own, including people, places, things, and events. When we vibrate faster and at higher levels, we attract new and higher experiences. The higher your vibration, the closer you are to the heavenly ethers and the more light and love you'll attract into all areas of life. The word "charisma" is derived from a root word meaning "Christ." We recognize people with a high vibration as being charismatic. They have a powerful magnetism. Love and positive vibes are irresistible.

- Meditation can eliminate racism, separatism, and elitism. We each look wonderfully different on the outside. Each person's "earth clothes" are unique, and there is a spectacular beauty in the variety of human beings. When we are in meditation, we are in communion with the Spirit within. Each human being has divinity at the core, which is our eternal essence. When we touch our own core essence of divinity, we see with new eyes. We see with a spiritual eye. We see the divinity in every human being regardless of the earth suit the person is currently wearing. No matter what the natural eye tells us, we are all the same within—divine and powerful—made in the very image and likeness of God.

• Meditation can keep us young. If you were able to remain calm and stress-free, stay mentally positive, be forgiving, have mental and emotional strength and fortitude, live a fully inspired life, reach your goals, fulfill your potential, live with passion and purpose, and do it all while remaining joyful, loving, kind, and happy, you would be well on your way to living a lengthy, healthy, and fulfilling life.

Though I am familiar with the benefits of meditation and have experienced all these and more, I am by no means a master, though that is my aspiration. I continue to apply myself to the practice and discipline of quieting my mind. Sometimes the mind chatterer doesn't cooperate and I have to wait a little longer for internal stillness. I am learning to be patient. I am learning to deep-breathe longer than the mind chatterer can last. After I spend sufficient time simply focusing on my breath, the mind chatterer calms down. I give her permission to rest. I allow her to take a nap.

With that said, if you'd like to begin a meditative practice, the question may be: *how do I meditate*?

To keep it simple, let's focus on three facets of preparation for successful meditation:

1. Prepare the environment. It's critical to a successful practice that you have a space that is quiet and relatively clear of stuff in order to meditate. It doesn't have to be fancy; a chair in a quiet, clean, and clear space is fine. Make sure the temperature in the room is comfortable. Make sure the room is quiet. If there are other people in your home, let them know when you'll be meditating (in advance) and set a firm boundary that they are not to interrupt you. Place items in the environment that bring to your mind the awareness of the presence of God, such as a candle.

2. Prepare your body. Wear loose-fitting clothing. Sit comfortably in a chair with your back straight. Put your feet flat on the floor. Place your hands in a palms-up receptive position or any other position that feels right for you. Take several very deep, slow breaths with your mouth closed. Breathe in and out slowly and deeply through your nose. Do this for several minutes. It may take twenty minutes or longer for the mind chatterer to calm down or for you to feel calm. Be patient. Be gentle.

3. Prepare your mind. You can start your meditation session by stating a powerful intention to have a positive meditative session during which you quiet your mind and feel your oneness with God. Remember, your mind entertains so many thoughts at once that it's necessary to train it to let go of mental busyness in favor of mental stillness. This mental training does not happen immediately. It is a process. Breathing helps to prepare your mind. Allow your mind to focus solely on your breathing, in and out, for several minutes to give your conscious mind an opportunity to shut down. It will do so after a long period of focused attention on anything repetitive. It's almost as if your mind becomes a bored little kid who can't stand to look at the same thing over and over again. After about twenty minutes of focused attention on your breathing, in and out, in and out, you'll feel your conscious mind start to slip into a quieter and more subdued mode. When thoughts arise, don't fight or resist them. Whatever you fight stays with you. Simply release your thoughts by letting them drift away easily. Ask for God's help.

Meditation is a practice and a discipline. It is an opportunity to focus your attention inward to the place within you where the Holy Spirit resides. You are proactively seeking to connect with your still, small voice of guidance, wisdom, and love.

In meditation, we come fully present to the Presence of which Abraham spoke: ". . . the Lord, in whose presence I walk." Meditation teaches us to walk in the presence of the Lord.

God's deep, unconditional, and ever-abiding love for you was the compelling influence that created you as a temple for the Spirit of the living God. Give quiet and focused attention to this thought each day and watch your life blossom.

Hush. Be still. You are now invited to be present to the Presence.

Thoughts for Today

Today, I am present to the Presence.

I silently revel in the tranquil love of God.

In moments of peaceful repose all things become clear and I come to know all is well in and with my soul.

I am a temple for the living God.

Inner peace brings a peaceful world for me and all my holy siblings on planet earth.

I am happy and serene on the inside, making my world happy and serene.

Love is all there is.

I am love and I am loved.

Today, I am tranquil and peaceful.

Nothing disturbs my blissful serenity.

Amen.

Re-Choose

"Lord, how many times may my brother sin against me and I forgive him and let it go? Up to seven times? Jesus answered him, I tell you, not up to seven times, but seventy times seven!"
Matthew 18:21-22 (AMP)

"Forgiveness isn't easy, but it's imperative."
Marianne Williamson, *"The Meaning of Midlife"*

When you make a mistake, which you do often, you can always choose again, for an unlimited number of times. It's a relief to know we have an unlimited account with God. Our Creator is not counting every little mistake you make, nor is God holding them all against you. There's no sin tally book in heaven.

God made you with the power and freedom to decide; to choose your own path. Though we're guided in advance about which paths lead to happiness and which lead to sorrow and pain, we remain completely free to take any road we choose. Each time you arrive at the proverbial fork in the road, you get to choose yet again which path you'll travel. Thankfully, guidance is always present and force is always absent.

When you choose a path that doesn't serve you well, or one that causes pain and/or suffering to yourself and others, take heart. You can always make another choice the next time around and know God is there for you no matter how many times you make a poor choice.

It's called forgiveness.

Forgiveness is both boundless and limitless with God.

I heard an example which illustrates the difference between God's unconditional, infinite capacity to forgive, and the limited way human beings tend to forgive. Picture it this way: when you make a mistake, or choose poorly, it's as if what you did gets written on a chalkboard. The offense could be as simple as telling a little lie, or as serious as committing murder. Whatever the offense, you get the opportunity to look at it, to review and consider what you've done. You get to experience the consequences. You then get to determine if the negative pattern you've created is one you'd rather not repeat.

When we learn from our mistakes and we desire to choose differently going forward, releasing patterns that don't serve us or others, we can choose to forgive ourselves, and bask in knowing that we have already been forgiven by God.

When God forgives us, our mistakes are erased from the chalkboard. The chalkboard is washed clean. All evidence of our mistakes is wiped from the slate by God's great forgiving hand. We start off fresh again, with a clean slate. This is God's promise.

Unlike God, when we say we've forgiven someone, we haven't always wiped the board completely clean with that person. What we have fallen into, maybe on more occasions than not, is to pick up the chalk and draw a line through others' mistakes (crossing them out) rather than completely erasing them. We leave other people's mistakes visible on the chalkboard of our minds and hearts. We even choose to revisit the chalkboard and review what's there every time we see the person. We have not disassociated the person from the mistake we've written on the chalkboard. The person and the chalkboard of mistakes have become one. This is the trap of unforgiveness: the chalkboard with all the mistakes written on it is only in your head, probably to the complete oblivion of the person with whom you're interacting.

God's forgiveness is maximal. You don't have to beg for it. You already have it. Every time you make a mistake. No matter the gravity of the offense, God's forgiveness is always assured.

God's forgiveness is limitless. Humans think in terms of numbers, like Jesus' disciples, who were looking for a number when asking Jesus how many times they were to forgive. How many times is my brother to sin and I keep forgiving him? How much is enough? This is such a human question. The tiny ego mind thinks in terms of limits. The question implies we come here with a set number of allowable offenses, and when those are used up, no more forgiveness can be extended. Like three strikes in baseball and you're out. They wanted to know what the number was for heaven. How many times do I keep forgiving?

Jesus, being a masterful teacher, knew what they were getting at. I believe his reply was intended to stretch their minds and hearts to be in harmony with God's idea of forgiveness: unbounded and unlimited.

The question is not one of God's forgiveness. More accurately, the question is: can you forgive yourself?

Mentally and emotionally wallowing in mistakes is both unnecessary and unloving. Living in regret over past deeds, replaying them over and over, is a destructive cycle that creates deep levels of guilt and shame. Continually beating yourself up over the same old things creates a negative recurring pattern, virtually ensuring you'll stumble in the same place again.

When self-flagellation becomes a habitual pattern, forgiveness is in order. Forgiving yourself is a compassionate path to self-love, and gives you the internal fortitude to stand up and make better choices the next time around.

Break out of the patterns of yesterday. Release shame and guilt by choosing to remember God's unconditional forgiveness, which is forever present. Then take a deep breath and forgive yourself. Let yourself off the hook. Be kind to yourself. Love yourself.

God's forgiveness is maximal at all points. Though you may not be able to escape the negative consequences that are tied to negative decisions and choices, you always get yet another chance. For instance, if you commit murder and have been found guilty in a court of law, you will most likely be punished by the state or country where you committed the crime. You know, from your own internal sense of morality, which some refer to as conscience, that you've made a grave mistake. You may spend much of your life in prison in unfavorable or dehumanizing conditions. These can all be counted as the negative effects which flow from your choice to take a precious human life. You cannot escape consequences.

However, there is a difference between suffering the consequences of your actions, and being forgiven by God. These are two completely separate events. God's forgiveness is assured. You may feel that since you are suffering through some pretty horrific consequences, you must be under God's punishment for transgression. You may feel God hasn't forgiven you.

There's a clear distinction between forgiveness and consequences. There is a balance of every action in the Universe. Each action carries a reaction. You will feel and live the effects of your choices, even though forgiveness is assured. Never feel God has withheld forgiveness from you because you're suffering consequences of your actions. We reap negative consequences when we sow negative thoughts, words, and deeds. Are you right now living through painful consequences of past poor choices? Once again, "Be still and know ye are God." Decide today to make better choices in each moment based upon divine guidance. As you consistently choose more wisely than you have previously, the consequences of your past poor choices will diminish and the positive results of your beneficial choices will start to appear.

Remember, God always allows U-turns.

You can always choose again. You are always assured of another chance. No matter how much humans despise what you've done, no matter how badly you may feel about your past misdeeds, no matter who you've hurt, you always get another chance. *Always*.

God loves you so—you are forgiven completely, fully and unconditionally, for all mistakes and errors.

Can you forgive yourself?

Thoughts for Today

God is in love with me—I always get another chance.

Today, I move forward with the quiet assurance that I always get to choose again.

God allows U-turns.

Today, I bask in the light of God's unconditional love, and I choose to compassionately forgive myself.

True forgiveness is infinite.

I am learning from all my choices, and I choose wisely in each moment based upon guidance.

Today I make better and better choices so as to experience better and better outcomes.

I am a child of the Most High and Almighty God— I am always assured of God's love and forgiveness.

Hallelujah.

Forgive

"And we know that God causes everything to work together for the good of those who love God and are called according to his purpose for them."
Romans 8:28 (NLT)

"Love, compassion, and forgiveness—these are the things I preach."
His Holiness the Dalai Lama

Thank God for your parents and caregivers.

If they were wonderful parents and caregivers, thank God.

If they were the parents and caregivers from hell, bless them and thank God that you survived.

If they abandoned you, bless them and thank God. Who knows what would have happened to you had they stayed?

If they abused you, bless them and thank God you're still here, due only to God's grace and unconditional love. You're still standing—what a gift you are to the world!

No matter what kind of parents and caregivers you've had, thank God for them and bless them. They were critical to your growth and development. It's largely because of them that you find yourself where you are today, even if you feel that where you are today is not where you want to be.

Your parents and caregivers had a heavy charge placed upon them when you were born. The charge was to take care of you and to provide unconditional love, wisdom, shelter, discipline, boundaries, support, and to give you a foundation upon which you could build your best life. They were called upon to answer your every call and cry for help from the second you were born. They were called upon to wake up in the middle of the night and stay up as long as you decided you wanted to stay up. They were called upon to bathe, clothe, and feed you, and to lovingly teach you to do it all on your own. They were charged with meeting your stages of development—including your difficult stages—with care, love, and patience. They were given the charge to grow you into being a productive, responsible, loving, compassionate member of society who contributes unique gifts and talents to the global family. They were called upon to nurture you: mind, body, and spirit.

Your parents and caregivers may have done all of this with excellence, or they may have been the worst you could have gotten. The reality is: there's not a perfect parent on the face of the earth. No parent who has ever lived has been able to do everything "just right." Every parent has made mistakes. Some of the mistakes were major, so major that they inflicted lasting emotional, spiritual, mental, physical, and/or psychological pain on their offspring. Some parents were just clueless and had no idea of how adversely their actions could or would affect another human being, especially a little one.

Some parents were completely absent or so derelict in their duties that they left room for others to take advantage of their young.

If you believe your parents met their charge and were outstanding at it, congratulations.

If, however, you are like the overwhelming majority of people I talk to, you fall into one of the following three camps:

1. You feel your parents and caregivers didn't do it "right," which resulted in discomfort and some pain. You feel you've gotten over it, but things could have been much better. The truth is, you're still hurting.

2. Your parents and caregivers were abusive and inflicted harm upon you, which resulted in much emotional, spiritual, psychological, and physical pain and distress. You're still hurting.

3. Your parents and caregivers were absent, neglectful, inattentive, drunk, or high on drugs. They knowingly or unknowingly allowed others to prey on you because they couldn't or wouldn't protect you from the unacceptable behavior of the people around you. You're still hurting.

You may even feel that your parents and caregivers were guilty of all of the above.

Here is a magic question for you: are you ready to heal those past injuries and move on? Even if you don't know how it can happen, do you desire healing for yourself, and are you willing to begin the journey toward healing these old traumas?

In the movie *The Lion King*, Rafiki whacks Simba on the head with a stick. When Simba loudly protests, Rafiki says, "It's in the past." Rafiki swings his staff and whacks Simba on the head a second time. When Simba yells again, Rafiki answers with the same statement, "It's in the past." Simba begins to get the point. What is in the past is in the past. When Rafiki swings his

staff a third time, Simba wisely ducks and misses
what could have been the third blow to his head.
He demonstrates his understanding in that instant. Though his past was painful, he garnered
the lessons from it and moved forward successfully, with less pain.

If your past includes people you consider hateful, ugly, unloving, unkind, uncaring, harmful,
mean, or abusive, your challenge is to begin to
heal those hurting parts of yourself by coming to
an understanding that the past is the past.

Today is today.

The question is: what will you do today?

Here's a radical idea for you: forgive them
completely. Forget about what your parents and
caregivers did yesterday. Develop a case of divine amnesia.

Right now you may be thinking, "I'm not
about to forgive and forget what they did to me!
It was hurtful and it terrified me and I was only
a little kid! They never apologized to me or even
admitted that they did anything wrong—I can't
just forgive and forget!"

There is a path that invariably leads to inner
peace: it is the way of radical, complete forgiveness followed by divine amnesia.

This path may require intensive healing work.
However, when you consider the alternative—

holding on to the pain of yesterday—it becomes clear that complete forgiveness and divine amnesia are your only peaceful solutions.

Here's another reason to forgive your parents and caretakers for what they did to you (or neglected to do for you): you're an adult now. They can no longer continue to do to you now what they were able to do to you then. Now, you have a voice, even though you may not have had a voice when you were little. Now you have choices. When you were little, you either didn't have choices, or if you did, you weren't aware of them, or, if you were aware of them, you may have been too afraid to exercise them. Now you hold the power over your life, unlike when you were a child. Now you are responsible: able to choose a response. Do not allow yourself to continue to respond to your parents—and the memories of what they did or didn't do—with lack of love, resentment, grief, bitterness, hatred, or unkindness. Choose now to have a different response to your parents and the memories you've been carrying around.

For you to arrive at the destination of radical, complete forgiveness, it may be helpful to understand more fully the nature of forgiveness and its true purpose in our lives.

Let's look at three ways we easily get off course with regard to forgiveness, and consider what the truth really is:

1. We think those who have hurt us should come to us and acknowledge exactly what they've done wrong. We want them to come to us and admit what they did to us and the error of their ways. What's more, we want an explanation. We want to know why they did what they did. We waste good years waiting for them to come back to us with an admission of guilt and a reasonable explanation for it all. In the meantime, we've picked out a set of luggage large enough to hold all the past pain. We've packed the luggage with all the old scenes in which we were hurt. We've packed in the luggage all the old stories of what happened. Since we didn't have any explanations, we had to create them. We've packed those too: all our made-up reasons for why they did what they did. We've got every inch of every crime ever committed against us packed in that set of luggage that we carry with us everywhere we go. We've made the abuse and neglect part of us, part of our story, part of our lives. It goes with us everywhere we go. We've even joined a group that consists of other people who have similar crimes packed in their luggage. We've even adopted a name for our group that makes us stand apart from the rest of the population who hasn't experienced this particular kind of pain. We get together frequently and talk about the crimes that were committed against us, which gives us all the opportunity to open each piece of our collective luggage to look at each crime over and over, lest we should forget (God forbid) even one of the gory details.

The truth is:

If you're awaiting an admission and an explanation from anyone—not just parents and caregivers—who you feel has done you wrong, you're treating yourself in an unloving way. Why? For two reasons: most people don't really know why they did the things they did. A negligent or abusive parent could not reasonably be expected to explain their unkind and unloving behavior. You're asking a person who doesn't have the answers to give you answers, and that is not likely to happen. Secondly, even in the rare cases when parents do know exactly why they did what they did, are you really expecting them to come clean and confess it all to you, their child? This is another unrealistic expectation and a setup for failure. There are not many parents who will voluntarily sit their kids down and fully detail to them why they did what they did, in all its horrid detail, and then beg the child's forgiveness. This scenario happens so rarely it is almost nonexistent. While you are busy lugging behind you that heavy set of baggage containing all the past crimes committed against you, the perpetrators of those crimes are off somewhere living their own lives.

Note: While you may want to join an organization that provides support for you on your healing journey, be careful about labeling yourself as a child of this or that disorder. Some members of support groups tend to put on a badge that separates them from the rest of society. People with similar pains tend to cluster together and review the pain. This is not healing. You are not what happened to you. You are not your parents. You are a divine child of God. Remember who you are and remember whose you are.

2. We think our attackers/abusers/punishers/neglectors should ask for our forgiveness. We tell ourselves that they haven't asked for forgiveness, so why should we extend it? We tell ourselves that they haven't even admitted their guilt, nor have they become repentant, which just proves how unworthy they are of our forgiveness. We tell ourselves that an apology must precede forgiveness. So we anxiously await others to apologize to us for the wrongs we feel they've committed against us.

When there is no apology (nor regret nor repentance that we can see) we think there can be no forgiveness.

The truth is:

Most people who have hurt you will not apologize to you (some of them don't believe they've done anything out of order in the first place). The sooner you realize and accept this, the happier you'll be. If you need an apology from someone, anyone, you can never be happy because you've given the power to create your happiness to someone else. Needy people are dangerous people, to themselves and others. As long as you need an apology from someone, you are needy and dangerous to yourself and to others.

This is also a matter of humility. The truth is: we are not owed any answers or apologies. We are not owed anything at all from anyone.

3. We think forgiveness is for the person to whom we are extending it. We believe that forgiveness is something we can decide to grant or withhold, like handing out candy. As long as we withhold forgiveness, we believe (somewhere deep inside) that we are making the other person suffer. We want them to pay for what they did. We're not ready to let them off the hook quite so quickly. We expect that after a person has admitted their full guilt to us and begged us for forgiveness, they should be happy, relieved, and jump for joy that we've decided, out of the kindness of our heart, to forgive them.

The truth is:

The forgiveness you decide to allow yourself to feel within your heart is not for anyone except you. Forgiveness is a way of life and is always and only for the person practicing it.

Forget about what your parents and caregivers did yesterday. They may be dead and gone, while you're still lamenting over what happened while they were alive. Choose to respond with love, forgiveness, and compassion.

Forget about what your parents and caregivers did yesterday. Let them off the hook. When you do, you let yourself off the hook too.

Forget about what your parents and caregivers did yesterday. Your doing so doesn't sanction their actions, nor does it mean you agree with them, nor does it mean they won't have consequences. Forgiveness simply means you release them and yourself from the mental and emotional hold they have on you. ***By letting them go, you set yourself free.***

Radical, complete forgiveness, along with a case of divine amnesia, are peaceful and self-loving options.

Further to this—hold onto your seat as you read this—forgiveness need only be extended to yourself. You forgive yourself for judging yourself as less because of what happened to you. You forgive yourself for carrying around a set of baggage that had grown to be unmanageable. You forgive yourself for all the times you reviewed the contents of those bags and horrified yourself all over again as if the crimes had just occurred. You forgive yourself for believing that you were shameful for anything anyone else did to you.

Forgiving yourself is a key to happiness.

It pays to remember this truth: *everyone is doing the best they can at the moment.* This may not be an easy concept to stomach, especially when it comes to an abusive childhood. It may help to know the only reason people behave the way they do is because that's what they know to do at the moment. They don't know any better. If they did, they would do better.

Let's consider the example of a parent who harbors anger and unleashes it on his child(ren) in the form of verbal and physical abuse. Let's further suppose this parent has an alcohol addiction. When under the influence of alcohol, the parent responds with explosive anger. Underneath it all, there are unhealed issues of anger, resentment, fear, and/or unworthiness. He will not likely desist in his destructive behavior until these issues are acknowledged and addressed. He may know, on an intellectual level, that he shouldn't beat or yell at his kids, however, when he's triggered, unresolved issues surface and explode dangerously, resulting in verbal or physical abuse perpetrated against the most innocent, vulnerable, and impressionable members of the family.

So, while a parent knows better—on a mental level—than to beat or yell at her kids (and she may even feel deeply remorseful afterward), when put under pressure, she responds in explosive ways because of her own internal, unresolved, uncontrollable rage, which has become a pattern in the subconscious mind and in the body. This person doesn't know better on a deep level, he or she doesn't know better on a body level, or on a cellular level.

The lesson here is simply this: you don't truly "know" something until it lives in every cell of your body. For the parent who's angry, he knows—on an intellectual level—that he is to love his children. However, on a cellular level, on the level of the subconscious mind, and on the level of emotion, anger is still raging. The anger will continue to surface each time the parent is triggered, even if the trigger is insignificant. An angry person responds to and interacts with others in angry ways. Knowing what to do intellectually doesn't override one's emotional patterned responses. The patterns of response that such a parent has built up have been solidified over time. Each time the pattern is repeated, it becomes stronger. The pattern will continue until the parent deems a change is necessary.

The complete and lasting solution to healing ourselves mentally, emotionally, and physically is spiritual transformation, which remakes us in totality from the inside out. When our very being is transformed, cellular change takes place. When cellular change takes place, we release the programmed ways we respond to stimuli.

When such a parent recognizes her need to change, and she is willing to submit to the Holy Spirit, she will be completely remade; mind, body, and emotions. New productive patterns will emerge and old patterns will disappear. You may have witnessed such a transformation in yourself or someone you know. The person undergoing the transformation may even look different than they did previously.

Everyone is simply doing the best they can based upon the habitual reactions which are lodged in the emotions, subconscious, and the cells of the body.

This leads us to the next reason why forgiveness is a self-loving choice (hold onto your seat again): the pain others inflict on you has nothing to do with you; it has only to do with what is going on inside of that person in that instant. This may be hard to believe, because when you feel you are being attacked, it does appear that the person is directing his anger and rage at you, and, in that moment, you may feel deeply affected, targeted, or even victimized.

There is a favorite quote of mine from the book, *A Course in Miracles*: "*In reality, you are perfectly unaffected by all expressions of lack of love . . .*

Peace is an attribute in you. You cannot find it outside."

What does this mean? Within you, there is a place of perfect peace. Within you, there is a place of tranquil stillness. Within you, there is a place where all good resides. Within you, there is a lake of absolute contentment and an ocean of unsurpassed love. Within you, there is a space so full, so loving, so perfect, that when you touch it, you imagine you are touching God. Indeed you are.

When you take yourself to this perfect place within you, you will see that this part of you is perfectly unaffected by any expression of lack of love. This perfect place within you is perfectly unaffected by verbal abuse, physical abuse, rape, incest, deprivation, starvation, lack, fear, greed, dishonor, and every other expression that lacks love. This place knows only God, and is indeed the image and likeness of God within you.

Consequently, while your conscious mind has clear recollection of all the expressions of lack of love, your deep, true Self is perfectly unaffected by it all. And while you may have carried the painful baggage around for years, and looked at it frequently, the truest and highest part of you has remained perfectly unaffected.

Your charge is to close your eyes and become quiet enough, long enough to touch that perfect, peaceful, contented God-space within you. The methods are meditation and prayer, as discussed previously in this work.

There's more—and perhaps this will cause you to see your suffering from a different and higher vantage point.

At the beginning of this chapter you were asked to bless parents who may have abused you. You also saw a quote from Romans, which states: All things work together for the good of those who are called according to His purpose.

The reason you are called upon to bless it all is because all that's in your life—and all that's ever been in your life—has worked together for your good. You may not have recognized the good in the midst of the pain, yet the good was ever present.

Today, ask God to show you all the ways you're a better, stronger, more resilient, and resourceful person because of what you lived through. Trust God to show you how your every painful experience can be what enables you to rise like a phoenix and triumph over it all.

God was watching over you all along; you were being fortified in the very moments when you considered yourself to be completely alone. You were never completely alone, and now you know it for sure.

One final word about the path of forgiveness and divine amnesia. You may say after reading this chapter, "That's all fine and dandy, but you don't know what I've been through. You don't know what they did to me. I don't feel any forgiveness in my heart toward the people who destroyed my life. I can't just let go of it." Can you start with the feeling of *willingness?* Your willingness provides an opening for the Holy Spirit. Affirm to yourself: *I am willing to forgive.* Pray stating your willingness to forgive. Share with God your heartfelt desire to feel better, to release the heaviness on your heart. Then ask to be shown the way. State this simple yet powerful prayer: ***Dear God, I am willing to forgive. Show me how. Amen.***

The beauty of God's unconditional love is that it can transform a seed of willingness, no matter how tiny, into a mighty tree. Looking at the size of an acorn, it's amazing it grows into a mighty oak tree. A mighty oak of forgiveness can grow from a tiny seed of willingness. There is nothing else you need do now. Stay willing and keep praying. God will do the rest. God will soften your heart and mind. Your willingness to forgive is the doorway to miracles.

I once heard that for us to be happy, we must forgive everyone for everything, especially and including ourselves. When we see the light of God's love, the dawning shines upon us and we know, in the light of truth, that there's truly nothing to forgive.

God is in love with you, ever-present, right by your side, even when you feel you're suffering. God can turn all your suffering into reasons for rejoicing. God's love for you is so all-encompassing, so full, that it calls us to put down all the heavy bags we've been carrying. When we do, we allow the Holy Spirit to free our minds and hearts through forgiveness.

You don't need to carry that load anymore. You are free now. Free to fly high.

A Forgiveness Prayer

*Holy One, Creator of all, I laud You, I praise
You, I honor You, I trust You in me.*
*Holy One, I trust in You and in the divine out-
working of Your perfect plan for my life.*
Holy One, I trust You even when it hurts.
*Holy One, I trust You and your perfect will,
even when I feel abandoned.*
*Holy One, I trust You and your promise, You
have never left my side.*
*Today, Great Redeemer, You redeem my soul
from the fire of fury.*
*Today, Great Redeemer, You redeem my soul
from the ashes of discontent and despair.*
*Today, Great Redeemer, You redeem my soul
from all that is not of You.*
*Today, Great Redeemer, You redeem my soul
from hell on earth.*
*Today, Mighty Jah, You walk with me in the
garden of perfect peace and stillness that lies
within my soul.*
*Today, Elohim, You guide me through pastures
of green grass, where I find rest for my tired
and weary bones.*
*Today, Adonai, You take me under your mighty
wing and I find shelter from all that would
haunt and torment me.*

Today, Lord of Hosts, You draw me and I fling myself into your bosom where my soul finds bliss, rest, and peace.

Today, God Almighty, You call me and I answer; I come running back to You and I throw myself into your loving, wide-outstretched arms.

Today I forgive and release all who have afflicted me. Today I forgive and release all whom I have viewed as tormentors. Today I forgive and release all whom I have judged as angry and full of rage. Today I forgive and release all who made me quake with fear. Today I forgive and release all who treated me with disdain, disregard, dismissal, and disrespect.

Today I forgive and release all who pressured, threatened, and coerced me to do things I didn't want to do.

Today I forgive and release all who lied to me, cheated on me, and stole from me.

Today I forgive and release all who abused me, raped me, beat me, and spoke curses upon me.

Today I forgive and release all who hated me.

Today I forgive and release all. All. All. They owe me nothing and they are now free to go.

I bless each one on their journey and know that God walks with each of them just as God walks with me, for each one of them is me.

Today I forgive myself for believing that I was alone, unwanted, and abandoned. Now I choose to walk with God.
Today I forgive myself for thinking that God is dead.
Now I know that God is alive and reigns with power in all my affairs.
Today I forgive myself for cursing God.
Now I praise God with all my mind, with all my heart, with all my soul, and with all my strength.
Today I forgive myself for believing that since God saw what was happening to me and if He really cared, He would have instantaneously stepped in and rescued me.
Now I know that all things work together for my good, and because God didn't step in every time to rescue me, I am stronger, wiser, bigger, better, and bolder.
Today I forgive myself for being so bitter about what happened to me, and for infecting others with the disease of discontent and bitterness.
Now I choose to be happy, joyful, triumphant, and victorious, and I infect others with happiness, joy, and victory.
Today I forgive myself for being angry and nasty and mean and hateful and ornery.

Now I choose to be full of love and compassion, and to express it always and in all ways.
Today I forgive myself for feeling like I had to figure out why things happened to me.
Now I choose faith, and it instantly negates any need I have to figure it out.
Today I forgive myself for secretly wanting to track down all the dirty dogs, lying mongrels, and snakes in the grass that did me wrong, and hurt them and slay them.
Now I choose to trust and know and surrender.
Today I forgive myself for not loving myself fully, totally, completely, absolutely, dramatically, inspiringly, creatively, positively, absolutely, exceptionally, and unconditionally.
Now I choose to dip myself into the ocean of God's love and be immersed in it.
Today I forgive myself for not inviting and allowing God's holy spirit into the deepest, darkest cracks, crevices, corners, crawlspaces, alleyways, hideouts, and recesses of my being.
Now I choose to invite and allow the holy spirit of the Almighty Living God to infill and indwell every inch of me.
Today I forgive myself for all. All. All. Just as God has already forgiven me. Now I choose to be still and know that Ye are God.
Amen

Grace

"Let us therefore approach the throne of grace
with boldness, so that we may receive mercy
and find grace to help in time of need."
Hebrews 4:16 (NLT)

"Faith is a living, daring confidence in God's
grace, so sure and certain that a man could
stake his life on it a thousand times."
Martin Luther

There is only one way for us not to experience
the fullest extent of the consequences of our
poor choices and negative actions: *by the grace
of God*.

There are two distinct ways grace manifests
for us.

One way God's grace shows up in our lives
is in increased strength and endurance to push
through negative consequences we experience as
a result of our poor choices.

Grace gives you peace in the midst of pain; it gives you warmth and comfort when the world around you is cold and unforgiving. Grace infuses you with dignity to hold your head high and press forward to a new day with trust and confidence. Grace is God's way of helping us through whatever consequences we're facing, even when the mess we are facing is of our own creation. Grace is that special something extra from God that urges us forward on the path to freedom. Grace is the extra lift, the gust of wind in our sails when we've been discouraged, beaten down, or traveled a painful path.

God's grace also offers a reprieve, almost like time off for good behavior. Though you may have committed a misdeed that could have resulted in serious and painful consequences, grace lessens the hurt. It mitigates the painful consequences. In addition to God's forgiveness, grace provides us with the opportunity to not have to fully suffer all negative consequences of our actions. If God's forgiveness is cake, grace is the icing. It makes the cake that much sweeter and delectable. God's grace is what's left after all else fades away.

God's grace is unconditional and extended freely to all. Grace, in the form of a reprieve, has affected every one of us after making serious mistakes. God grants reprieves every day.

You may have had several reprieves in your life already. Know that you'll receive countless more before you leave the planet.

God granted King David a reprieve. There is a story in the Hebrew scriptures of the Holy Bible about King David and his poor choice to conduct a census of the nation even though he was not to do so. David, like each of us, had free will. He chose poorly. After realizing and confessing his misdeed, his conscience began to bother him. He called out to God for forgiveness. God sent the prophet Gad to David to tell him he had three choices of what he could suffer as a consequence. The options were: three years of famine in the land, three months of running from his enemies, or three days of an epidemic in the land. David responded that he didn't want to run from his enemies, as they would probably not have mercy on him. He said that he would rather leave the outcome to God, who has mercy and extends grace, rather than to be placed in the hands of humans.

David, knowing the power of God's grace, made a wise choice in choosing his consequence. He said: "I am in great distress. Let us fall into the hands of the Lord, for His mercies are many *and* great; but let me not fall into the hands of man." (2 Samuel 24:14, AMP)

Consequently, an epidemic came upon the people. According to the story, the angel of God stood between heaven and earth with his sword outstretched, and the people died in large numbers. There were strong outcries and entreaties to God to stop the epidemic. The prayers to God worked. God, in His grace and mercy, told the angel He had sent to halt the killing.

As a result, the fullest extent of David's consequences did not get played out. David and the nation were granted a reprieve. God extended grace to David and to Israel.

I view this story as a reminder of God's forgiveness coupled with God's grace. God's forgiveness is assured, no matter how many destructive patterns we create with negative thinking, poor choices, and negative actions.

However, even though God's forgiveness is assured, we still experience the negative consequences of our negative behavior and poor choices. Sometimes the consequences can become so burdensome that we wonder if we'll make it through.

When the consequences of your negative thinking, feelings, attitudes, and actions become almost unbearable, ***pray for God's grace, and you shall have it.***

Grace is a lifesaver. It is most active when we know we've strayed off course, possibly hurting ourselves and others in the process, and we're facing consequences that could be severe. Just then, God steps in with grace, and instantly, we can be in a place of peace. Grace is extended to all, always. Pray for God's *grace*.

You've probably experienced the grace phenomenon on several occasions. Maybe you were at the wrong place at the wrong time and found yourself in a dangerous and frightening situation. You came out of it unscathed, though you know you could have been hurt or even killed. God's grace stepped in, right on time. We land ourselves in precarious positions; yet, grace comes in and saves the day.

Perhaps you were lying on your deathbed and you aren't anymore. God's grace stepped in, to the rescue. Perhaps you lost your mind, and now you have it back. God's grace did that too. Perhaps someone close to you transitioned out of this life and you thought you'd never survive. Yet you're still standing. God's grace appeared, once again.

Know that forgiveness and grace go hand in hand. They will help you survive anything.

And know that, when the painful consequences of your negative actions show up, God's grace is right where you are.

Today, pray for God's grace.

Thoughts for Today

God's grace surrounds me and grants me peace always.

God's grace grants me holiness always.

God's grace brings me love on the wings of angels always.

Today, my mistakes, fears, and insecurities melt away in the ever-flowing river of God's mercy, forgiveness, and grace.

I am the grace of God made manifest.

Thank You, God, for grace.

Companions

"For He will give His angels (especial) charge over you to accompany *and* defend *and* preserve you in all your ways . . ."
Psalm 91:11 (AMP)

"Your own personal angel, who was with you when you were a little baby in the crib, and will someday be there at your deathbed, is now watching you read."
Anthony DeStefano, *A Travel Guide to Heaven*

In the moment you agreed to come here, God assigned constant companions to you. God's instructions to them were clear: no matter what happens, they were to never leave your side. They were told to protect you, to give you guidance and support, and if you didn't pay attention the first time, to use an infinite array of avenues to get your attention. They were told to send you inspiration and creative ideas that would make your life better and richer. They were told to help and support you, without doing your work for you. They were also carefully instructed to never, ever interfere with your free will, no matter how destructive your choices.

When they received their instructions, they agreed to all of the demands of the job. If doing the job meant working overtime, they agreed. If it meant performing on-the-spot miracles, they agreed. If it meant allowing you to go through painful learning experiences, even though they had the power to stop it, they agreed. If it meant going into the darkest places in the world after you, they agreed. They agreed to go with you wherever you went, no matter how dark, no matter how sinister, no matter how frightening, no matter what; for your entire earthly existence.

Beyond all that, they were happy to accept their assignment. They rejoiced at the thought of spending your earthly life with you and the opportunity it gave them to serve God. They were excited about the assignment to guard you in all your ways and to inspire you to live the life God imagines for you.

Perhaps you've known folks who said they'd never leave you, yet they're not in your life today.

Your companions have kept their promise. They're with you right now, having always been, and always will be, for as long as you live.

The companions I'm referring to are your personal team of angels.

They are the ultimate promise-keepers. They've been with you every second of your life here. They've never left your side.

Though you may have never seen an angel in your life, they are there. You may seriously wonder if angels even exist. Even still, they are there.

The life we live on earth can be difficult. When we came here, God knew we would need all the help we could get. He provided a vast ocean of resources for us when we were born, internal and external. One of the resources God provided to each of us was a set of angels—guardians and helpers—who would follow us everywhere, making our lives a little easier, saving us from grave danger and giving us inspiration and guidance.

Some religious traditions believe that we're each given two guardian angels who guard us throughout the day, and two who guard us throughout the night as we sleep.

Some believe we have two guardian angels around us at all times.

Some believe we're surrounded by invisible spirit helpers, a team of guardians and guides.

Whatever your belief about angels, it doesn't matter. They are there. You don't have to believe in them for them to do their job. They believe in you. Your team of angels doesn't carry out their job based on the amount of faith you have in them or in God. Your angels have been, and are now, loyal to you and are by your side until you pass out of this human life. Nothing you can do can make them go away. You can't scare them away. You can't yell them away. You can't push them away. You can't command them to leave you. They are there, by your side, right now.

The word "angel" means "messenger." When you're very quiet, you can hear them speaking to you. This is how you benefit most from your team of angelic guides and guardians. Allow them to speak to your heart. Allow them to bring you messages of hope and comfort from God. Allow them in, so they can have their way with you. Allow them to do what is highest and best in your life, as they are always acting in the interests of God's will for your life. Allow them to guide you by listening to the voice of wisdom within. Allow them to protect you.

How do you allow your angelic team to help you?

By knowing you have mighty, supernatural help in all you do. Act like you know you have a powerful team of miracle-working, God-sent spirits with you every second of every day. Just moving through life with the awareness that you're not alone has the power to re-shape your perspective. When you know, to the core of your soul, that supernatural help, guidance, and protection is ever present, at your beck and call, your life takes on an immediate and permanent change for the better. When you hold this full awareness, there's nothing anyone could say to you that would devalue or frighten you.

I want you to try an exercise. Close your eyes and picture the following:

Imagine an enormous mighty angel, 20 feet tall, with a flaming sword, standing just behind you on your right side. Now picture another enormous mighty angel, 20 feet tall as well, with a scepter in hand, standing just behind you on your left. How does that mental image make you feel? If you remembered these two beings in everything you did, all day long, do you think you would proceed through life differently? Just knowing they are there gives you an assurance and peace that defies description.

Most of us make up stories about life that are not beneficial, such as "life is hard," "life is one long uphill climb," or "nothing worthwhile comes easy." Rather than creating mental stories that are disempowering, create mental images and ideas that inspire and empower you. Even if there were no such thing as angels, it is empowering to create mental images of them anyway. Whatever is in your head happens in your life. It's all consciousness. Believing in your angelic hosts is equivalent to having a consciousness of empowerment, which elicits feelings of being supported and well taken care of.

You always have choices. You can create a consciousness of being alone, unsupported, and having to do everything yourself, or you can create a consciousness of being supported, safe, and so fully loved by God that there are benevolent beings ready to do good on your behalf. Holding mental images of your angelic companions is one way to create a consciousness of being fully loved, supported, and gifted with all the natural and supernatural help you'll ever need. It's all right there for you. You don't have to go looking for anything. All the help you'll ever need is right where you are, right now. This consciousness is empowering.

The love of God is such that hand-picked spirit beings have been dispatched to you, who have only your best interests at heart, who've agreed to be ever present, who've promised to protect and defend you, and who desire to inspire you to be who God created you to be, and to do the wondrous things God sent you here to do.

This is pure love.

There's more.

In addition to the angels that are with you at all times, when you're going through particularly difficult times, God often sends additional angels to bolster you for as long as is necessary.

God sent His angels to minister to the needs of Jesus after his forty-day fast in the wilderness when he found himself in a weakened state. When you're in a wilderness situation, feeling as if you are barely existing, know and feel the presence of God's angels at your side, ministering to you in the midst of the barren desert. Stay alert and aware, learn your lessons quickly from the experience, and allow your angelic helpers to sustain you as you see your way out of the wilderness.

God sent His angels to shut the mouths of the lions when Daniel was thrown into the lion's den. When you feel you've been thrown to the lions and you fear you'll be completely devoured, know, just then, God's mighty angels are there, protecting you. The angels will deliver you from the mouths of lions just as they delivered Daniel. Allow them to rescue you from the thought of being eaten alive.

God sent His angel to help three young Hebrews—Shadrach, Meshach, and Abednego—who were thrown into the fire for their steadfast conviction and faith. When you're in the fiery furnace and all in life seems to be ablaze around you, know God's angels are there, walking in the midst of the fire with you to deliver you, completely unharmed, from the experience. Your angels can take the heat.

God sent an angel to free Peter from prison. When you feel stuck, chained, and imprisoned, with no way to break free, just then, God's angels are there to help release you from your mental, emotional, and even your physical prisons.

There's more.

God's angels are there when you've just come through a trying period, and you need continued grace and guidance.

God sent His angel to go before the Israelites after they'd been set free and had fled Egypt. The Israelites' story is not unlike ours. Oftentimes, after we've gained our freedom from enslaving conditions, we feel as if what enslaved us is still in hot pursuit. You've gained your freedom, yet you're still running hard and fast, hoping to escape your pursuer. Maybe you were enslaved to smoking. After having been free from the chains of cigarettes, you're still looking over your shoulder, haunted by the thought of falling back into the trap by smoking one cigarette. Or maybe you were enslaved to alcohol. Now that you're free, you know you're only one drink away from being enslaved again. Perhaps your enslavement was to sex. You've worked your way through it, yet you know you could fall down if you allow yourself to be in the wrong place at the wrong time. Maybe you were enslaved to fighting, arguments, and confrontation. Now that you've broken free of anger, you know to be watchful, lest hot-headed thoughts lead you back into slavery. We've all been enslaved. The particular brand of slavery doesn't matter. After we've overcome and gained our freedom, by the grace of God, we know we must continue our journey with vigilance and watchfulness. God's angels are there to guide our every step; protecting and leading us to our promised land and protecting us from ourselves.

Follow the path your angels have brightened for you today.

God's angels are there providing you with protection at all times. This doesn't mean that you'll never experience certain violent acts or tragedies. The angels are not there to render you immune from the pain of life; they are there to protect you from what is not meant for you to experience. They are the great mediators, they mediate and regulate life's experiences according to what God knows we are able to handle. No more will ever happen to you than you can absolutely handle with all God has provided. Remember, angels cannot and will not interfere with your free will and choice. However, they will step in and save your life, if need be and if it's not your time to exit yet. Think of how many times your guardian angels may have saved your life. Think of how many times you've been in situations where you needed protection, and help came, and you knew it was not the human kind. These are the experiences where we knew we were in danger and help came, seemingly out of nowhere and not according to human capability. What about all the times we don't know about that our angels have stepped in? I'm sure I've been in danger when I didn't even know it. If we're not aware we are in danger, we wouldn't know to ask for help. Isn't God's love awesome that we don't have to ask? Angels take the initiative and step in even when we don't know we're in danger. This is an awe-inspiring thought.

The angels who surround children seem to work overtime. I remember an instance, among many, when our son was in danger and his guardians stepped in. We were watching television, and little Ronnie was sitting on the floor right under the television with his feet up on the television stand. Because he was moving his feet, the stand shifted and the television toppled forward, yet, surprisingly, it didn't fall. It appeared that the only thing preventing the television from falling forward right onto Ronnie's head was the plug, which was still in the socket on the wall. We scrambled over and grabbed the television. To me, there was no way a television of that weight and size could have been prevented from falling by a plug in the wall. I remember having the distinct feeling that there was angelic protection around him just then. It was a supernatural moment.

Think of how swiftly God moves on your behalf by dispatching as many angels as you require for the situation you're in. In a split second, you're surrounded by all the additional supernatural help and protection you need. This has been happening for you the entire time you've been here, whether you knew it or not. Start now to pay attention. Notice all the ways you receive superhuman help exactly when you need it.

Another function of the angelic hosts is to provide you with the strength you need to move forward, even when you feel you're not able to take another step.

God's promise is clear:

> "But those who wait for the Lord [who expect, look for, and hope in Him] shall change and renew their strength and power; they

shall lift their wings and mount up [close to God] as eagles [mount up to the sun]; they shall run and not be weary, they shall walk and not faint or become tired."
Isaiah 40:31 (AMP)

God dispatches angels to give you the added strength and renewed vigor to keep going when you think you're too tired to take another step. God specializes in renewing us when we've reached exhaustion. It's in those times that we most need God, and it's in those times that help is near. There is no reason for us to do anything on our own. Unfortunately, we often exhaust ourselves, calling upon God only after we've lost all strength.

Remember, *help is always right where you are, in every instant you require it.* Whatever you need is miraculously provided for you, before you even ask.

When things are going well for you, the angels are there, cheering you on and singing your praises. Angels don't stand by idly until trouble appears. They congregate with you on happy occasions, too. When a child is born, angels appear to welcome that precious, beautiful new life to the earth; even if the child's parents don't feel the same way. When couples get married, angels crash the wedding! They're there to witness the sacred event, to sing beautiful songs of joy, and to amplify God's glorious presence at the nuptials.

The angels appear when you're rejoicing; they help you rejoice. The angels appear when you're happy, creating even greater joy within you.

Your angels are always with you. They're ever present, benevolent spirits who have agreed to protect, defend, guard, guide, uplift, inspire, encourage, sustain, and support you. They're right now surrounding you with God's unconditional love.

They're there to remind you of just how deeply you're loved and how truly lovable you are.

Your job is to simply be. Practice sitting in the silence, allowing yourself to feel God's love in every cell of your body. Allow your consciousness to be flooded with healing energy. Bask in the love emanating from your angels now. Know you are unconditionally loved by each and every angel. God created an uncountable multitude of angelic spirits. You are loved immeasurably by each and all of them.

Your angels want you to succeed. They want to see you triumph. They want to rejoice with you. They want to see you being used as a tool in God's hands to bring light and love to countless others. The angels want to catapult you to new and higher places.

No matter who you are, terrorist or priest, you have angels surrounding you with love, reminding you of your natural state of being, which is pure joy.

If you're having a challenge with drugs, your angels surround you with the light of freedom. They long for you to break free of your addictions and be the person God created you to be. Indeed, they stand ready to help you through your withdrawal. All you have to do is decide, and God and the angels will give you all the strength you need to break free and stay free.

If you're living the street life, not sure of who you are, you are right now surrounded by loving beings who want you to know how unconditionally loved you are. They send you love every day, and, somewhere in your soul, you feel it. It may be buried beneath layers and layers of pain and hurt, yet you feel that little twinkle of love. Know that that tiny bit of joy and love that lies at the center of your soul is expansive and can encompass your being completely and wholly, if you allow it. Your angels know how to rock you in their arms and blanket you with God's love.

No matter who you are, or what kind of life you live, you have angels at your disposal in every moment. They're with you continually, and when you pass out of this life, they'll be with you then, too, attending you as you cross to the other side.

When you consider what your angels do, and all that they do that you're not even aware of, the depth of God's unconditional love becomes increasingly clear.

The Holy Bible refers to God as the Lord of Hosts, also translated as Lord of the Angel Armies.

The Lord of the Angel Armies has provided you with mighty and powerful, benevolent beings who agreed to be your constant and watchful companions.

Now that's love.

Thoughts for Today

A team of God's angels stand on my left and on my right at all times.

Though I walk through the valley of the shadow of death, I fear no evil, for the angels walk before me, lighting my way.

The angels walk behind me, supporting me and protecting me from all harm.

Today, I remember that each and every angel knows my name.

Each angel loves me unconditionally, just as God does.

My guardian angels stand watch over my mind, body, and soul, day and night.

Today, I accept and receive love from my personal team of angels.

I am deeply joyful for the angelic hosts that surround me. I gladly and gratefully follow their guidance.

Ask

"Another angel, who had a gold incense container, came and stood at the altar. He was given a lot of incense to add to the prayers of all God's people and to offer it on the gold altar that stands before the throne."
Revelation 8:3 (GNT)

"The angels are here to help you heal your life, and they want you to ask for help."
Doreen Virtue, *Healing With the Angels*

A few years ago, I noticed I felt a supernatural presence in certain parts of the home I was living in at the time. There was never an actual sighting of another being; it was more a sense of an invisible presence that seemed to prefer certain spaces within the home. When I first felt the feeling, I didn't know what it was, or who. I simply had a feeling that someone, some entity, was there with me, somewhat reminiscent of my childhood experiences.

At first, I ignored the feeling, dismissing it as imagination and fancy. My logical, thinking mind didn't want to deal with anything it couldn't define or explain.

The feeling didn't go away; it actually intensified.

In the quiet of my home one night, while washing dishes, I felt the presence enter the room. It seemed to be positioned behind me. In that moment, I became more intrigued than ever. I was always curious about the presence whenever I sensed it, but I never did anything about my curiosity; my rational mind made sure of that.

This night, I decided to end my curiosity once and for all.

Who are you? I asked internally, wanting to know and not wanting to know at the same time. I didn't hear anything. My back was still turned to the place where I felt the presence, so I decided I wanted to turn around. However, I also knew I dreaded seeing anything supernatural, so I turned quite slowly and sheepishly, silently hoping not to see anything. The last thing I wanted was to turn around and see some non-human, terrifyingly huge spirit standing in the middle of the kitchen. Even if it was a good spirit, I told myself I wasn't ready for that kind of shocking experience.

When I completed my turn and didn't see anything, I was relieved.

Still not hearing anything, I inquired silently of the presence again, *What's your name?*

This time, there was an answer.

Damiel. His reply didn't reach me by way of an audible voice. I guess I would describe it as perceiving his answer. Now I knew for sure he was male, which I had previously only suspected.

Why are you here? was my next question, though it wasn't my real question: *what do you want with me and should I run?*

Then, without words, the presence emanated the greatest and most profound love I had ever felt. I stood there for I don't know how long, feeling quite heavenly and completely overtaken by love.

Now, as I reflect on that night, I suspect this being had been with me all my life. I also suspect that this love had been emanating from him toward me all along. That night, standing in the kitchen, with my full attention on the presence, I could at last feel the love that surely had been present all along.

That was how I first consciously met one of the angels who guide me, Damiel.

The next day, I got the bright idea to Google Damiel. I don't know how I came up with the idea to look up an angel on the Internet, but that's what my little human mind told me to do at the time, so I went for it. I must have known, on some level, the Internet could not have possibly told me anything about this presence that I couldn't have found out by just asking him. Hence, I got nowhere in my Web search. Nothing I found on the Internet corresponded to what I felt in the kitchen.

Damiel could not be defined or explained by a Web search.

Darn.

I realized in that moment the level of fear that must have been present for me in this whole experience. I say that because I inquired nothing further of the angel Damiel the night I consciously met him. Though I perceived nothing fearful about his presence, I sought explanations about him elsewhere, rather than having a communication with him. It was abundantly clear that he would communicate anything to me about himself that I wanted to know. I was too fearful to go there. In my mind, asking a question or two of an angel is one thing. Sitting down and having a full-fledged conversation over a cup of tea is quite another. Fear is a powerful thing. It kept me from finding out what I truly wanted to know about and from Damiel, which was everything. Everything like "what's heaven like?" and "what do you guys do all day?" and "does God really have a white beard?" You know, run-of-the-mill kind of stuff.

My fearful reluctance to have a conversation with the angel in the kitchen had a lot to do with my upbringing. I'll tell you how the fearful dread of spirits, even benevolent ones, began.

When I was about four years old, my mother decided to become one of Jehovah's Witnesses. A few years after adopting her new faith, she got married to a wonderful man, who was also one of Jehovah's Witnesses. I was happy; here was the father I'd always wanted. My mother and father raised us according to the doctrines and teachings of Jehovah's Witnesses, so ours was a traditional, fundamentalist Christian family. In our world, sightings of supernatural entities were strictly forbidden. Being able to feel or perceive supernatural entities was unfavorable, too. Any supernatural beings that would appear, according to my upbringing and religious conditioning, were most certainly demonic. News of such sightings were not welcomed. More accurately, they were downright dreaded. It was made overwhelmingly clear to me that people in modern times didn't "see things." Only way back when, in Biblical times, did people see angels. Only way back when, in Biblical times, did people see spirits of any kind. And that was okay then. But not today. That kind of thing just doesn't happen anymore. God communicates with people differently now, in this modern day and age. "If you see anything supernatural, Valerie, you can be sure it's one of the bad guys: the devil and his demonic hordes."

That was the story I was handed.

There were two very big problems with this story. For me, it didn't resonate intellectually, nor did it resonate on a deeper spiritual level of absolute knowing, which springs from personal experience. Let's examine both perspectives.

First, the story didn't seem to make much logical sense to me as a child. It left a host of unanswered questions: If I could see one kind of spirit, the evil ones, why couldn't I just as easily see the good spirits? Were the good spirits hiding? Did they all get together and agree not to show up anymore after the Bible was finished being written? Why? I didn't understand, so I verbalized my questions. I quickly discovered, in the world I grew up in, that persistent and unanswerable questions from children were often not a good idea. They were met with impatience, disregard, or the stern warning not to question God. Despite my doubts and queries about this theory, I eventually started to play along with the game, albeit on the surface. Besides, if I tell myself the same story long enough, I'll eventually believe it, whether it has validity or not. The story was repeated so often and adamantly that it began to wear away my resistance while gaining momentum and taking up more of my mental space. *After all,* I thought *the big people must know how the world works; they must know what they're talking about.*

The other big problem with the story: it was totally irreconcilable with what I knew within. And what I knew within—even as a child—sprung from my own experience. As a little girl, I remember perceiving powerful, benevolent energies, which I assumed must have come from another world. I remember knowing things without understanding how I came to know them. I remember looking at people and being able to see right through them. My mother's friends frequently told her to tell me to stop staring at them. It made them squirm when I stared at them. Most times, I was not at all aware I was staring. It was, now that I look back, the wonderment at what I saw. At other times, I remember waking up at night and knowing other beings were present in the room with me. Most times, their presence didn't matter to me one way or the other, unless the visitors seemed mischievous or ill-inclined. I recall one supernatural character who would show up frequently in my grandmother's house. He was tall, imposing, and wore all black, complete with a large black hat. From my childhood eyes, he looked quite menacing. I sensed he was not there for the good of all involved. Other than isolated events, most of my experiences with the supernatural were benign and none were harmful. It's fascinating to me how children seem to possess a clear sense of all worlds, both spirit and natural, without being worried or fearful. Children seem to know more about how the spiritual and natural worlds really work.

My sightings and supernatural experiences were commonplace and natural to me for the first several years of my life. It was only after the introduction of the new religious story that I came to think of the various entities who had been hanging around us as harmful and perhaps evil. That was the beginning of my internal worry and fear over what I was experiencing.

Yet, far beneath the story I was handed about seeing spirits, far beneath the beliefs I was given about the supernatural world, part of me was always consciously connected to the other dimension, to another world. Yes, beneath the story was a feeling and a knowing that I couldn't shake off.

Because my childhood experiences with the world of spirit didn't fit into my parents' carefully constructed paradigm of religious dogma or their concepts of how things worked, it left me in a state of inner conflict: *Do I continue to believe what my parents are telling me, or do I go with what I know and feel?* The conflict wouldn't go away, so I chose to ignore it.

Ignoring inner conflict doesn't resolve it. In this process, I learned a valuable and life-long lesson: my truth will insistently and consistently rise to the surface from deep within, seeking expression.

Even though I was a practicing member of my parents' religion for twenty years, the deep knowing within me about benevolent spirit forces never left. It never subsided. It was an ever-present knowing of the angelic beings at my disposal, joyful to supply me with whatever I required to do God's will. The deepest parts of me knew angels and other helpful spirit beings interacted with us on an ongoing basis and that it was all quite natural; one of the most natural things in the world. The part of me that was inherently and consciously connected to the spirit world never went away (nor could it), no matter how much I tried to ignore or suppress it in the name of religion.

After many years as a Jehovah's Witness, I came to a point where I knew it was not the religion for me. I began to actively rebel against their teachings and rules. I look back on my period of rebellion against what I had learned as my way of untying myself from that form of worship. I do recognize now that there were more graceful ways of leaving, without breaking the rules. Yet, my path has held priceless gems of wisdom for me. I am happy for my entire journey.

For years after leaving the religion of my parents, remnants of the conditioning lingered. During that period, two internally opposed energies— the box of beliefs handed to me by my parents along with the requisite amount of guilt about letting it go, versus my deep inner knowing from my own experiences with the spirit world—co-existed in an internal stalemate of sorts. For a long while, I did nothing about the stalemate. I took what I thought was the easy way out: I ignored the inner conflict.

During the stalemate/inner conflict period, I would come across reading material about the spirit world; much of which I could relate to because of my personal experiences. The books I was drawn to about folks who had seen angels and other spirits fascinated me and touched me at my core. The parental and religious conditioning was progressively lifting to reveal an inner light of spiritual knowing. Though I didn't need them to, I felt, at the time, that the books I was reading validated my experiences.

Then came the night I met Damiel. This angel of love offered me the golden opportunity to blast away the shreds of religious conditioning still hanging around in my consciousness. I was handed the opportunity, in that very instant, to fully release any and all remaining beliefs that didn't harmonize with my experience of the spirit world and my inner knowing. Not just some of them; all of them. That night, standing in the kitchen, the occasion arose for me to make a clear choice: hold onto the remnants of a belief system born out of religious conditioning even though it didn't agree with my spirit, or let it all go and open myself to fully embrace what I had known deep inside all along: there are countless benevolent supernatural forces working with and for me.

You get to choose, Valerie; you and only you. That was the offer on the kitchen table.

I chose Damiel. I chose to honor the truth within me. I chose to say yes to what I knew all along, without fighting, without resisting, and without trying to make the enormity of what I was feeling fit into a very small box.

Ever since I made that choice, I've been having the time of my life, being consciously supported by angelic hosts whom God has sent to guide, protect, and care for me.

Right now, a host of benevolent guides and protectors are encamped around you, ten-thousand at your right hand and ten-thousand at your left. A myriad more are at your disposal. Just ask. How loving must God be to send such powerfully benevolent beings to accompany us? This depth of love is unfathomable.

God is surely in love with you.

Thoughts for Today:

I am thankful for the angelic hosts encamped about me.

Today, I allow the angels to have their way with me—I surrender to their loving care.

I honor all the spirit beings God has sent to help me.

I honor my inner truth.

I know.

I live in harmony with what I know.

Thank you, God, for expressing your unconditional love for me in the manifestation of constant companions who are with me always.

Today I ask my angels and I listen closely for answers.

Thank You, God, for the blessings we call angels!

Feelings

". . . I am content and at peace. As a child lies quietly in its mother's arms, so my heart is quiet within me."
Psalms 131:2 (GNT)

"Heavenly Father, Thou art all feeling, will, and thought. Guide Thou my feeling, will, and thought; let them follow, let them be as Thou art."
Paramahansa Yogananda, *Scientific Healing Affirmations*

I got married in Hawaii on the island of Oahu. We stayed at an elegant resort on Waikiki Beach that overlooked the ocean. We had an ocean-front room with a lanai where we enjoyed the sights and sounds of Hawaii. Every morning we were awakened by a gentle breeze rolling off the ocean, and every night we were lulled to sleep by the calming lap of rolling waves. Because of the time difference between Hawaii and my home state of Maryland, I found myself waking up at 5:00 A.M. the first few mornings we were there, feeling energized and ready to hop out of bed. Upon arising, I'd go out on the lanai and entrance myself by watching the ocean and its early morning dance. It became a peaceful way to start each day in the Hawaiian paradise.

The first morning I was there, I saw what appeared to be heads bobbing up and down in the ocean. Squinting my eyes and jutting my head forward, I strained to see into the distance. As I stared out onto the surface of the ocean, I could make out people. Not swimming, or going anywhere, they were just hanging out in the ocean. I couldn't figure out what so many people would be doing bobbing around (apparently aimlessly) in the ocean at the crack of dawn. I inquired later about it and was told the folks I had been curiously watching and wondering about were surfers. They get up early in the morning, grab their surfboards, and position themselves at just the right place in the ocean, with hopes of riding the best waves a surfer could ask for.

Since I began to see that I wasn't going to sleep much past five o'clock in the morning during my stay in Hawaii, I decided to make the time productive. I began making a study of the Hawaiian surfers. I watched them as they bobbed around, patiently expectant. I watched them watch the waves advance toward them. Their anticipation and excitement when a large wall of water approached was almost palpable. When just the right wave came along, they'd jump up on their surfboards and take a stance, ready for action. Then they'd ride the wave all the way in, having the time of their lives standing on and maneuvering what appeared to be long pieces of brightly painted wood. I could almost feel their glee and excitement when they were riding high. What a blast!

When waves arose that didn't meet their criteria, they allowed the wave to pass by unceremoniously. No engagement. No activity. Just heads bobbing up and down in the water as the wave passed by almost unnoticed. I imagined that they were out there engaging themselves in quiet conversation when insignificant waves happened by.

Watching the surfers taught me many lessons, not the least of which is how to engage with the powerful emotions we carry around at all times, a perfect gift from our Creator. Our emotions are a signal and guide for us.

Earlier we discussed intuition as an internal guidance system that always provides necessary and valuable information. The feelings that guide us each day are a vital part of the continuous flow of communication from God. When we engage our intuition, we are led by God's voice speaking to us, many times through how we *feel*. We can use our feelings as a barometer when determining whether a certain course of action is appropriate for us.

When we feel wary or hesitant, there's a reason.

When we feel fearful, there's a reason.

When we feel happy, joyful, and elated, there's a reason.

Paying attention to how you feel provides you with valuable information.

Understanding your intuition and the unique way it expresses through how you feel is key to having a life you desire and coming to a fuller understanding of God's unconditional love for you. You are wholly loved, so you are never left alone to figure out what to do. You are being gently led, guided, and informed regarding every aspect of your life and every question that arises in every moment of every day.

You don't need to go looking for answers.

You already have all the answers.

All the guidance you'll ever need has its source within you right now. We seek answers externally when we already know what to do. We ask others what they think when we don't really give a hoot what they think; or when we already know what to do and are just too afraid to do it; or when we're looking for someone else to agree with us. Then we blame the person when we take their advice and things turn sour.

Either way, we always know what to do. You can feel what's right for you and you can determine what's not right for you by how you feel.

This raises the question about the legitimacy of feelings. We always know what to do, deep inside, but we don't always do it. Why? One reason is because we seek to legitimize what we're feeling by attaching an explanation or logic. The difficulty is that we don't always have a logical reason for how we feel; we just feel it. No logical reason is necessary when it comes to feelings. A rationale doesn't accompany feelings. Nor do your feelings need to be legitimatized. They are legitimatized by their very existence.

In my second marriage, I was feeling that it was time for me to exit the relationship. I didn't have a clear reason to explain what I felt, so I stuffed the feelings inside in a vain attempt at avoidance. Over time, the feelings didn't go away. Quite the opposite, they became more persistent. I didn't feel peaceful within. I was conflicted because I had a feeling and I wanted an explanation or a rationale for it. Since I didn't have a clear and full explanation, and I felt I needed one, I experienced inner conflict and unhappiness. It was not until I gave voice and recognition to the full range of what I was feeling that I reached a state of grace. I sat in the feelings and really felt them. I asked them what they were here to teach me. When it was all said and done, I came to greater clarity about what was really going on.

What I learned from the process was powerful: I invite inner turmoil when I don't give my feelings my full attention, recognition, and validation. My need to have an explanation or a rationale for how I was feeling—and my need to be able to present the explanation and rationale clearly and fully to others—actually worked against me and my desires for peace and tranquility in my intimate relationship.

You don't have to explain your feelings to anyone. Go with the flow of your feelings and emotions and trust that the full answers will materialize in due time.

Feelings are the spontaneous sensations that arise in the body as a result of thought. You cannot have a feeling without a thought preceding it. The range of feelings can include: uneasiness, distress, apprehension, frustration, being startled.

Emotions are spontaneous states of being, which can arise from a thought held in consciousness for a longer period of time. For instance, when you think of something that's frightening to you, the first startle you feel in your body is the feeling. As you continue to ruminate on the thought, you can actually work yourself up to the emotion of fear. You can feel startled without having the emotion of fear. However, if you continue to ponder what startled you and worry over what could happen to you, the feeling of being startled turns into the emotion of fear.

Emotions can also arise from simply being. These positive emotions arise from being in a meditative state where little or no thought takes place, where we are deeply connected to the divine within. Certain emotions—such as joy, bliss, and peace—are natural states of being. Other emotions—such as fear and anger—require us to work our way into these states.

Let's talk about the rules of engagement when it comes to feelings and emotions. These rules of engagement are designed to make your emotional inklings, surges, and urges pleasant, meaningful, and informative. Before the rules of engagement are stated, let us consider the following two ideas with regard to emotions:

- **All feelings and emotions are gifts.**
  The full range of human emotion is a gift,
  even emotions we label as negative, including anger, rage, jealousy, hatred, and
  resentment. All feelings and emotions are
  gifts because they tell us about ourselves
  and what's right for us in the moment. They
  cue us as to what's not right for us, too. God
  lovingly placed within us an internal system
  that gives us clear and powerful signals.
  What a gift!

- **You are the one who has control over
  your emotions at all times.** Quite a
  number of us have learned the detrimental
  habit of pinning the blame for our emotions on other people. I frequently hear,
  "She made me so mad," or, as my teenager
  is fond of saying (usually with reference to
  an authority figure or a recently dumped
  boyfriend), "He gets on my nerves!" or the
  proverbial saying often spoken by parting
  lovers, "He/she doesn't make me happy
  anymore." As we'll discuss in more detail,
  no one can make you angry or mad or happy. No one has the power or ability to force
  you into any particular emotion. *The emotions you feel at any given time are
  always your choice*.

As mentioned earlier, emotions are like waves in the ocean. And just as the surfers in the ocean surrounding Hawaii didn't engage and ride out every wave, realize that not every emotion arising within you is suitable for full engagement. Conversely, just as the ocean produces waves that are perfect for riding high, some of the emotions that arise within us are perfect to fully engage and ride high. Some emotions, if fully engaged, will uplift us. These emotions are love, joy, peace, gratitude, and others similar to these. Then there are the emotions that leave us feeling depleted and disconnected: anger, hatred, resentment, and others just like them. There are only two kinds of emotions: the ones that feel good and the ones that don't.

Here are the rules of engagement in managing our emotions. The key to managing our emotions is threefold:

1. **Become fully aware of all you're feeling in each moment**. Awareness leads to growth. If you're not aware of what you're feeling, there's no way you can improve on it.
2. **Accept whatever you are feeling in the moment**. Acceptance brings peace as it removes the need to fight or resist what is.

Accept everything about yourself in every moment, without shame or apology.

3. **Know that you can—and decide to— make a different choice the next time**. Increasingly engage in more and more of the uplifting "feel-good" emotions while gradually diminishing the "don't-feel-good" emotions. Make the conscious choice to feel good most of the time and then train yourself to do it.

How can you achieve all three objectives? To begin, consider the following as you become aware of, fully experience, and begin to transform your emotions:

1. When an emotion arises that doesn't feel good, allow yourself to fully experience it. Don't stuff it down, or try to hide or deny it. Give yourself permission to feel it. Feel it fully. Be fully in the moment with the emotion, whatever it may be and no matter how painful it may feel. There's a gem in what you're feeling; you simply need to find it.

If you're feeling agitated and become angry, know that you have the right to be angry in that moment. *Warning: if you happen to be interacting with other people in the moment you feel anger rising, temporarily remove yourself from their company so you won't lash out at or hurt anyone else. Though you have the absolute right to be angry, you do not have the right to subject other people to your angry fit.* Go somewhere by yourself and beat a pillow. Go into the woods and scream at the trees; they can take it. Nature has an uncanny ability to absorb negative states of being. Go for a vigorous walk or run. Do some push-ups. Shake your hands and arms vigorously. Shake your entire body. Express the energy fully without harming yourself or anyone else. Get it out of your system. Adopting this practice allows you to expend the anger energy without keeping it pent up inside the body, which could later lead to disease. Cancers and other disease states are the result of unexpressed anger and resentment that have been bottled up for years.

Remember, no one else is responsible for how you feel. How you feel is always your choice. While it's true that someone may have triggered an emotional response in you, that person is not the cause of your emotional response. The person did or said something, and, in an instant, you decided what her words or actions meant to you. You then reacted. It was all your choice. You chose what to think and feel about what the other person said or did.

Herein lies the reason we experience emotions that don't feel good: attaching a meaning to the words and actions of others. When we decide what something someone says or does means, we open the door to feeling bad. For one thing, the meaning we attach to events is, for the most part, negative. It's also, for the most part, completely inaccurate.

The minute you decide to stop assigning meanings to everything in your world, you'll start feeling better.

I'll give you an example. When I was young, an older relative engaged me in inappropriate sexual behavior. It happened on more than one occasion, and in those moments, I felt terrified and degraded. After each incident, I felt as if I were less than a full person. I felt dirty. Over time, I harbored doubts about my value.

I began to attach more meaning to the events, which gave rise to emotions that didn't feel good. I told myself I was less than a full person because of what had happened. I felt there was something wrong with me. I told myself there was something wrong with the person who committed the acts. I thought I hated the person. I didn't want to feel any of the feelings associated with the incidents, so I stuffed them in a box in the corner of my soul. I thought if I kept the lid on all the raw feelings inside that box, I'd be okay.

I could function well enough in life and no one would ever know. I could eventually forget the whole thing.

As it turned out, everything I told myself about myself was completely fabricated. The stories didn't make me feel good, and worse, none of them were accurate. I came to realize it wasn't true that I was less than a full person because of what I experienced. The truth is: it was an experience I had. Experiences don't define who we are. It wasn't true that something was wrong with me. Even though I was in mental and emotional pain, there's a timeless part of me that was never—and indeed could never—be hurt or denied. It wasn't true that I hated the other person. God's love and compassionate forgiveness point the way to love for all involved. We are each doing only what we know how to do in any situation.

It certainly wasn't true that I could just go on as if nothing had happened if I stuffed all my raw emotions that didn't feel good in a box and buried the box deep inside. The truth is, by stuffing all that raw emotion, I created an internal volcano. When it erupted, it spewed fire and ash everywhere and left a trail of destruction in its wake. I didn't feel good, nor did the people around me.

With regard to emotions, of this you can be sure: when you stuff raw feelings deep inside, you create an internal volcano. You will not be able to escape the heat and fire that will surely come to the surface.

None of my fabrications made me feel good, and they were woefully inaccurate. They all served to chip away at my emotional foundation, piece by precious piece. The erosion continued until I decided to drop all the stories in a radical healing act that occurred on a spiritual retreat. I was prompted by Spirit to tell my story. When God first dropped the notion into my mind, I balked. "No way, God. I'm not talking about that to anybody!" It's funny how we can argue with God, especially when God's guidance is for our eternal benefit.

Well, I was about to learn a valuable lesson: never say what I'll never do. Something happened within me and in my world, and just a few hours later, I found myself standing before a large group of people sharing everything. It was almost as if I were compelled, and there I was, talking openly and publicly discussing the deepest secrets I had carried for years. Part of me felt like I was watching another part of me. It was almost as if I were watching myself in a movie scene.

It was a powerfully healing moment. In an instant, I dropped the stories I'd been telling myself for decades. When I sat back down, I felt as if a 1,000-pound weight had been lifted from my chest.

Since then, one of my most profound life lessons is this: when I give meaning to events, I invite emotions that don't feel good.

The antithesis of making up my mind about what things mean is asking, *what is the lesson here for me now?* When you're in emotions that don't feel good, instead of fabricating a story about what the other person meant and what it means about you, feel the emotion fully. As you do, ask yourself:

- What is this emotion here to teach me?
- What am I learning about myself right now?
- How old was I the very first time I experienced this feeling? What was happening? What did I tell myself about what was happening? What did I tell myself about myself in that moment? What did I tell myself about the other people involved?

When we give ourselves permission to fully feel our emotions, we get to discover the gem that lies within that emotion. There's a gem in every emotion. When we sit in it and inquire, the gem always comes forth.

The next time you experience emotions that don't feel good, stay fully present with the feeling and ask God to show you what the feelings and emotions are there to teach you. You're being offered guidance in that moment. Ask what the guidance is. Ask and the gem shall be given to you.

This same process applies to emotions that feel good. When you're experiencing emotions that feel good, notice what you're doing. Notice what's happening. This too is a valuable insight for you in sustaining emotions that feel good. Being happy accidentally rarely happens. You must be the conscious creator of a happy life. Don't expect happiness to happen by default. You can learn to become happier every day by learning what truly gives you happiness.

Ask yourself what makes you happy. Is it:

- A walk on the beach? Then walk the beach more often.
- Playing with your dog? Then make sure you play with your dog every day and for longer periods of time.
- Painting? Then paint a little more than you are now.

- Connecting with friends and family? Then plan to connect with friends and family more often.
- Doing nothing? Then fill in several appointments on your calendar to "do nothing."

Learn yourself well. Learn what makes you happy. Learn what brings you immense joy. Explore and discover yourself. You're going on a quest for invaluable information that will serve you for the rest of your life. It will make your life's experiences richer and fuller. You'll know what keeps you in joy and you'll do it more and more.

Remember, God loves you unconditionally and wants your unconditional happiness, just as much as you do. You're the only one preventing you from being happy. If you remove your unwillingness to be joyful, you'll automatically return to your natural state of happiness and joy in living.

2. After you've allowed yourself to fully feel all your feelings and emotions and you've asked for the gem in every life experience, the next step is total acceptance. Accept where you are and what you're feeling. Do not exit a feeling and berate yourself for having the feeling. We beat ourselves up over our feelings, which is anti-transformational. The feeling exists. Honor it. Accept it. Honor yourself for having the strength to face it and be in it. Accept yourself while you experience the emotion, then after the emotion has subsided, without beating yourself up for having the emotion.

Give yourself permission to feel whatever you feel, when you feel it, without feeling guilty or bad about it. In the first step above, you allowed yourself to feel the emotion fully and you asked what the emotion is there to teach you about yourself. Now, you're allowing yourself to feel the full range of emotion with complete acceptance, sans guilt. When you fully accept yourself and whatever you're feeling in the moment, you're freed from social norms that prohibit authentic emotional displays. Society has taught us when to laugh and when to cry according to what is deemed "acceptable." We've been carefully taught, and we've learned when to hurt and when to feel good. None of these social norms may coincide with how you're truly feeling in any given moment.

Looking at children and what they do can be liberating. I was at a funeral for a dear aunt not long ago. When we arrived at the cemetery after the funeral, the children who were with us (and there were many, as our family has lots of kids) seemed to have the idea that they were at the park. They weren't sad. They wanted to run and play. They picked flowers like they were in a garden. They laughed. It was refreshing to watch. The adults were sad, partly because we were saying good-bye to the physical form of Auntie and partly because we've been conditioned to be sad at funerals. It's what society has taught us is acceptable to feel at such a time. Other emotional displays at a funeral would appear out of place and unacceptable.

However, Auntie had lived a full and eventful life, and was quite a jokester when she was alive. She kept us laughing most of the time. Somewhere inside me, there was a part of me that was rejoicing over a life well lived. Many a humorous memory with Auntie came up in my mind, and some of the memories tempted me to chuckle. I didn't. I looked around seriously and considered everyone else who was present. I have been conditioned to be sad at funerals, even when it may not be completely inappropriate to chuckle at a funny thought involving the person being honored. We've been taught that funerals are a time for tears.

Well, the kids didn't feel that way. None of them cried. They had fun. As far as they knew, they went to church and then they went to the park and picked flowers. They had a beautiful day while the rest of us were either eulogizing Auntie or agonizing over her.

Taking odds with social norms doesn't mean we don't have consideration for those around us. It simply means we give ourselves permission to feel whatever we're feeling in any given moment without being hemmed in by what we think we should be feeling. Give up what you think you should feel, which, in most cases, has been dictated to you, in favor of acceptance of what you authentically feel.

Give up, once and for all, all of the following:

- "I wish I didn't feel this way."
- "I never want to feel like this again."
- "I don't know why I feel like this."
- "I feel so bad."
- "I shouldn't feel like this."
- Say this to yourself instead:
- "I am okay with how I feel right now. I am learning from this experience."
- "I am praying to find out what lesson is here for me so that I may learn it and move on."
- "I explore my feelings to see from where they arise, and I faithfully ask God to show

me how to heal those parts of myself that don't feel good."

- "I don't feel good right now and I accept it. It is what it is. I ask to see the gem that's surely present in this."
- "I ask and I receive. I know I am now being shown what this feeling is here to teach me."
- "I love myself and I allow myself to feel whatever I am feeling without 'shoulds,' blame, or guilt. There's no shame in my game!"

Self-acceptance is the path to peace. God loves you unconditionally and accepts you unconditionally. Why give yourself any less?

A word of caution: self-acceptance doesn't mean staying stuck. There's a great divide between accepting yourself and growing, and staying stuck and deciding not to grow. Acceptance means we know we're walking a unique spiritual journey of healing. Anyplace we find ourselves on the road is perfectly okay as we continually love ourselves into moving forward. Staying stuck means we refuse to grow, learn, and transform. The former leads to freedom, the latter leads to stagnation and eventual death. Nature is efficient about doing away with anything that doesn't serve the greater good, including people. Have you noticed that people who sit around and complain seem to age faster than people who are proactively engaged in making their lives better? That's because the law of nature says we have a choice: contribute or be recycled. There are only two choices: transform and grow, or rot and die. We're either growing into bigger beings or we're decaying into death. It may take years for nature to dispose of you if you've made the choice not to grow, but the decay is happening.

Accept yourself and your path as you continue to move forward, with a mound of self-love and self-appreciation.

3. Once you've spent time discovering and learning yourself, decide to be happy. Decide to do what makes you feel good most of the time. It sounds easy, but we all know people who don't feel good most of the time. You may be one of them. If you are, just decide to do something different. This process works even if you already feel good and would like to feel even better. The decision to feel good most of the time is enough to get you moving away from emotions that don't feel good and toward emotions that do.

Decide to make a conscious choice the next time you're entertaining emotions that don't feel good. If you're not feeling good, choose instead to feel good. You are always at choice. You have free will at all times. You're in control of what you choose to feel. Up until now, you may have been acting unconsciously and simply repeating old patterns of behavior without thinking. Now you know, if you are to be the conscious creator of a life you love, you will have to fully exercise your ability to choose. You're now choosing to no longer unconsciously react; you are now choosing to consciously respond.

By making the choice to respond differently, you initiate the change process. Just by virtue of your new awareness of yourself and what you do, which is Step #1 above, and your self-acceptance, which is Step #2, you're now moving to a new level of self-awareness where you begin to see the issues inside yourself. No one else can make you feel any emotion; you choose to feel what you feel. You know what triggers you and why. You know your emotions are valuable teachers and you've decided to be a willing student. You've proactively chosen growth and transformation over stagnation and death. You've been praying for new eyes, to see God's divine healing plan for your life (which has been unfolding all along whether you were aware of it or not), and for the willingness to actively engage in that wondrous and miraculous plan.

The most powerful ways to initiate and sustain transformation are through continual prayer and meditation. Pick a time and set an appointment with God. Pick the time of day when you'll be at your best. It may be early in the morning. After you've set your appointment with God, show up. Be on time. Bring a heart and mind that are willing, ready, and able to surrender. Get quiet. Be still. Do nothing. Just be. Take a few very deep breaths to cleanse and clear. When you've sat quietly for a while, speak to God. Share with God the depth of your love and adoration. Share with God your awareness of divine activity in your life and in you. Share with God that you've relinquished control and you've completely surrendered yourself. Share with God your complete reliance on the Holy Spirit. Allow your heart to pour out in thankfulness to your Creator. Ask God how you might continue your healing journey and how you can feel better. Ask God to show you what to do, and share with God your willingness to do it. Then, be willing to do what you feel your heart leading you to do. The first few messages you receive from the Spirit may be frightening, like my experience of being led to share a secret I'd been carrying for years. All along the way, be assured of God's unconditional love and absolute commitment to you and to your healing. God wants you whole, healthy, and healed.

When you've finished sharing with God, write down any thoughts or inclinations that come to you. You may want to record these thoughts and feelings in a journal that you save for reading and reflection later.

This gentle daily process of spending time in the company of the One who loves you unconditionally is healing in itself. If you already have a daily appointment with God, now is the time to expand it. Deepen it. Broaden it. Allow it to move you to a new, deeper level. We're never finished with our spiritual work, as long as we're alive. That's the yummy part: that we never finish. We can always grow. We can always be—and reach for—something better.

You'll notice after days, weeks, months, and years of spiritual practice that your emotions become transformed, and you'll find yourself feeling good most of the time. Spiritual practice is not a guarantee against negative feelings and emotions. It is a guarantee that you'll feel better, and when you don't, you'll know how to return to feeling good.

You are human. Part of being human is experiencing the full range of feelings and emotions. All emotion is a gift.

Our Creator has lovingly provided the Holy Spirit as a helper that heals diseased mental states, which lead to emotional trauma or upsets.

Accept God's unconditional love today. Allow it to wash over you and cleanse painful feelings and old injuries. Then be filled with happiness sublime and joy unbounded. This is God's promise. Enjoy.

Thoughts for Today

I feel good!

Today I give myself permission to feel whatever feelings and emotions arise, without shame, guilt, or apology.

I accept things as they are. It is what it is and it is all good.

I learn from every emotion.

My emotions are teaching me valuable lessons about myself and I am a willing student.

Thank You, God, for healing my heart.

Relationships

"Oh my love, how beautiful you are! There is
no flaw in you!"
Song of Solomon 4:7 (AMP)

"We are as attracted to love as we are intimidated
by it. We are motivated by love, controlled by it,
inspired by it, healed by it, and destroyed by it."
Caroline Myss, Ph.D., *Anatomy of the Spirit*

I was sixteen years old when I met my first
husband. He was fine and I was enamored. Seven years later we were married. Thirteen years
after that we were divorced.

In 1996, I met my second husband. He was attractive and I was attracted. Eight years later, we
were married in a beautiful sunset ceremony on
a beach in Hawaii.

As of the time of this writing, I am, once again,
separated. The good news is: we've decided to
reunite. I've committed this relationship to God,

who will surely work it out. I am doing what I know how to do: pray and follow the leadings of the Holy Spirit as best I can at every turn, as I continue to lovingly work on me.

It may seem strange, it does to me anyhow, that I would be writing about the meaning of relationships, considering that the only two significant romantic relationships I've experienced thus far didn't turn out as I had expected. From one perspective, both relationships could appear to have been major challenges, with one ending in divorce and the other coming dangerously close to it. I know otherwise. Both relationships were—and continue to be—outstanding and life-changing successes.

After spending the last thirty years of my life involved in significant love relationships, I've come to some understanding of the real meaning of relationships. I don't have it all figured out, that's for sure. And, apparently, society and the people who taught me about love didn't have it all quite figured out either. That's okay. We're all learning and growing. In the process, there are some landmark lessons I've learned that I'd like to share. My lessons may make your life walk a little easier; they've certainly been an eye-opener for me.

1. I was taught that love and marriage are supposed to last forever. We're supposed to find someone, get married, and live happily ever after, or at least until "death do us part." The idea sounds good at first, but it doesn't seem to work out this way in real life. I know people who have been in relationship with each other for a long time. Sadly, some of them are missing the "happy" part. Then, there are people who are happy in relationships for a time, but miss the "ever after" part. It seems that most people are not able to manage a "happily ever after" relationship.

I believe it may be because we start relationships with an illusion; therefore the relationship becomes based on illusion and not truth. The truth is, we enter relationships to learn and grow. We are in relationship with another to become more like God and less like who we were when we first started the relationship.

In order for us to learn and grow, there must be significant challenge: challenge to what we thought we believed, challenge to how we behave, and challenge to our perceptions of self. The idea is that God uses our relationships as sandpaper: creating friction to smooth out the rough spots. If each of us started our relationships based upon this truth, not illusion, perhaps more of us would reach "happily ever after."

2. Since relationships are for learning and spiritual growth, it seems to follow that we may not be in relationship with the same person for life. We may, and we may not. It depends. It depends on both partners and where they are spiritually and where they each desire to be. When each partner is intentionally working internally to become more like God, the relationship may last a lifetime. If one partner is committed to spiritual growth and development and the other partner isn't, the relationship may be a lot shorter. Either way, each partner will learn valuable lessons in the process if they are each open to the notion of growth and transformation.

3. If it holds true that relationships are for learning and spiritual growth and they may not last a lifetime (although they can and may), there's something else to consider. As is learned when each partner is committed to his own or her own spiritual growth and development: each person is responsible for the relationship. All of it.

This is a bold statement, I know, and I'm still working with it myself. I don't fully understand it on a logical level, though I can fathom it on a deeper spiritual level.

To make it easier, let's look at an example. Suppose I'm in relationship with someone who breaks our mutual commitment of fidelity, and has sex outside the relationship. Let's also suppose that the infidelity happens repeatedly over a period of time. In this scenario, it would be easy for me to look at my partner and blame him for philandering. It would be easy for me to leave the relationship and blame the whole thing on someone else. I would probably talk to friends and family about it, most of whom would probably see my point. I would become a vindicated victim.

The real question here is not why my mate broke a commitment. The real question is: *what within me is causing me to attract and be in relationship with someone who breaks commitments to me?* Or, put another way: *how do I break commitments to myself?* The answer to that question yields the true reason why I find myself in relationship with someone who doesn't honor commitments.

The only way I can be in relationship with someone who doesn't honor commitments to me is if I don't honor commitments to me. The person in the bedroom with me is only acting as God's holy mirror at the time. God shows us what we do by bringing people into our life experience that do the same things. It's God's ingenious way of getting us to pay attention, heal, and grow.

Sadly, we often miss the message. I've missed this message—and the resulting lessons—more times than I can count. I'm still apt to miss it on days when I may not be thinking clearly. I look at other people and the stuff they do and blame it on them. Then God lovingly brings to my mind something my mom used to say: "Whenever you point your finger at someone else, just remember there are three fingers pointing back at you." Blame never works and is, therefore, totally useless. No one who gets blamed for anything likes it and rarely do they own up to it. So what's the point of blaming anyone for anything? After all, everyone in my life is here by my invitation, either consciously or unconsciously. Since this person is present, there are many lessons to be learned from the relationship.

One of the most important lessons is: my mate is being used by God to show me what I'm thinking and feeling about myself, about life, and about God. My mate is here to show me what all my unhealthy stuff looks like and what I need to release. My mate is here to show me all the things about myself that I don't want to look at and have either conveniently forgotten or have blatantly dismissed. You can run, but you can't hide. Say it with me: *my mate is my mirror*.

4. If relationships are for learning and spiritual growth and they may not last a lifetime, and my mate is my mirror and blame never works, then another truth must follow: there's only one person I can manage, control, and change in all my relationships: me. This wasn't an easy pill for me to swallow. I'm still working on it. My current husband does certain things that I would love to wave a magic wand and make disappear. He has grated on my nerves in more ways than I can count. Though I love him, I don't always like him. I am learning the lesson that there's nothing I can control or change about him. It's not my job. Even if I wanted to take it on as a job, I'd be doomed to fail.

God made me to be able to change and control myself, and each person is made the same way: to control only self. Each person has full freedom of choice and the will to exercise the power of choice. We each have freedom to do as we please. There are consequences in all we do, yet we're free to choose what we think, say, and do.

In light of God's beautiful gift of free will, I must respect my husband's choices. All of them. I do not agree with all of them. I think some of them are absolutely ridiculous. I think others are just downright dumb. I think others are life-threatening, like his recent motorcycle purchase. None of that matters. It's not for me to make his choices for him; neither is it loving for me to attempt to do so.

Because God's gift of free will is weaved into the very core and essence of who we are, any attempt to control another or keep his will suppressed will be met with eventual resistance. No human is made to be controlled by another. It's why no instance of slavery has been able to stay in force forever. No dictator lasts forever. Control by another naturally goes against the grain of human dignity.

Though we cannot control everything that appears in our lives, we are responsible: able to choose a response. I am here to control one person: me. I can change only one person: me. I can be used by God to affect change in others, and I am happy to do so. Yet, I am clear that it's God who does the work and I can change no one.

This awareness leads to peace. If we can see each person as an autonomous child of God, free to choose what they will, we can let go of trying to make other people do what we want them to do. We can let go of control. We can let go of manipulation.

5. This doesn't mean we allow our mates—in the midst of exercising their free will—to do anything they want in our presence. Being in control of myself means consciously deciding what is and what isn't okay with me while I am in relationship with another. While I cannot choose for another, I can choose what another will do around me. I am always at choice, just as my mate is. While a mate may be choosing a certain course of action, I am free to make my own choices about that action.

My most recent relationship was with a mate who chose to smoke. I choose not to smoke. I also choose that smoking will not happen in my presence. I cannot stop another from smoking, yet I can choose to be in a smoke-free environment at all times, and I can make that happen for myself. Since my mate is my mirror, his smoking is a reminder to me of the self-destructive activities and behaviors in which I engage. The message and lesson for both of us is to quit self-destructive behaviors, however they manifest. One person may do it one way and another person does it another; it's all the same. Remember, we are always at choice. Always.

6. Considering all the foregoing, my most valuable lesson from the past thirty years is to focus my attention on one thing: my own spiritual transformation by actively, consciously, and intentionally engaging in a life commitment to my spiritual growth, no matter what else does or doesn't happen.

Prayerfully, my lessons of the past thirty years encourage you to commit to you. Whether you're in a relationship that's wonderful or not, commit today to your own spiritual growth, development, and transformation. Your relationship with God and your relationship with yourself are the most important relationships you'll ever have. You will only attract to yourself who you are. You can only change what you attract when you change who you are. As your relationship with God deepens and broadens, you will attract supportive, loving relationships. The more you learn to love yourself, the more you will attract others who love you just as you love you.

I am open to God's guidance as to how my most recent relationship will turn out. It may be transformed into a relationship that supports both of us wholly. That would be wonderful. It may turn out otherwise. That remains to be seen. Either way, I learn and grow. God knows what's best for me. I've given up trying to figure it all out myself.

Know that God is in love with you—so much in love with you that you've been provided relationships with people who look, think, act, and speak just like you. It's God's most loving way of getting you to see what you really look like. Look at your mate and look in the mirror; God's holy mirror.

Thoughts for Today

My relationships feed me.

God shows me what I look like by using the people closest to me.

I am grateful for these "holy mirrors."

The grace of God is in the midst of all my relationships.

I allow harmony to reign in my intimate relationships.

I am in love with me, which makes it easy for me to radiate love.

I love God.

God's love is all I'll ever need.

Equanimity

"And there are distinctive varieties of operation,
but it is the same God Who inspires and
energizes them all in all."
1 Corinthians 12:6 (AMP)

"There are profit and loss, slander and honor,
praise and abuse, suffering and pleasure in this
world; the Enlightened One is not controlled
by these external things; they will cease
as quickly as they come."
The Teaching of Buddha

Equanimity is defined as evenness of mind,
especially under stress; right disposition; balance.

For me, it means treating everyone as they
are: a blessed child of God. No one deserves
special attention more than another. No one
is more important than another. There are no
people who have more significance to God than

others. Each one of us is different, no better or
worse than another. There's no range of value
with regard to human beings; meaning, there are
no human beings who are more valuable to God
than others. We each have intrinsic value. You're
priceless. It's the value God endowed you with
when you were created.

You are God's idea of who you are.

In the Eastern part of the world, there is a
principle that represents not being unduly affected by what people think, say, or do. It's called
not being blown by the eight winds. The eight
winds are: profit and loss, slander and honor,
praise and ridicule, suffering and pleasure.

When considering two of the eight winds, praise
and ridicule, the idea is for us to keep a centered
and steady state of mind whether we're being
praised or ridiculed. Either way, both praise and
ridicule are opportunities to stay grounded in
God's idea of who we are, not someone else's idea
of who we are.

Some of us are overly affected by praise. When
someone praises us, we may begin to think of
ourselves as being better, or superior. I've done
it, and remain prone to doing it if I hear too
much praise without keeping myself grounded.
Part of me wants to hang on every word of the
compliments being offered and savor each syl-

lable. That part of me wants to revel in the intoxication that may accompany lavish praise.

Then there is the part of me that is unduly affected by ridicule and criticism. When I hear negative feedback, I tend to get upset, to go into victim thinking and behavior, or I may want to lash out at the offending party. That part of me doesn't like being criticized and lets it be known.

The principle of the eight winds teaches me to remain centered in God's idea of who I am, whether in the face of lavish praise or searing criticism. Whenever I feel tempted to allow my internal peaceful state to be bloated artificially by lavish praise or to be deflated artificially by sharp criticism, the eight winds idea serves as an excellent reminder. I can choose to remember my value as being set by God, and that it is not affected by the vicissitudes of human thinking. What people think of me could change in an instant. What God thinks of me is eternal and everlasting. I choose to remember that I am God's idea of who I am.

Equanimity means staying in a peaceful, God-centered state on the inside, which creates a peaceful, divine state of being in all of life's affairs.

Equanimity also is, for me, the realization that no one deserves to be on a pedestal. I've noticed my tendency to put others I deem as highly accomplished on a pedestal; a practice that is unfair to the other party and to me. How can I expect someone else to live up to the height and weight of a pedestal I've created? How can I live up to the height and weight of a pedestal someone else has created (in their mind) and put me atop? The person who's on the pedestal may not even be aware that she's up so high in someone's imagination.

Inevitably, I've found that whenever I had an exalted notion or idea about someone, once I got to know him more intimately, he became just another human being on a journey of discovery. Just like me. There was nothing special, nothing extraordinary; just another child of God doing what children of God do. I would arrive at the conclusion in a judgmental way, when the person did or said something that I judged as being "beneath" him. Or, as my mom would say, when the person's "true colors" started to show. It was precisely at that moment that the individual in question fell from the pedestal I'd carefully crafted for him. In a split second, he'd made the long descent (only in my mind) from artificially inflated importance to the sea of normalcy.

Have you noticed that when folks don't live up to the image we've mentally created for them, we get mad? Or perhaps we feel disappointed. Most of the time, they never asked us to put them on a pedestal anyway. That was our call. It's best to not create pedestals in the first place, and see each person for who they truly are: a divine child of God, no better and no worse.

In putting away my habit of creating pedestals, I am likewise learning to let go of my scintillation at discovering that someone may have me on a pedestal. We know when folks have an artificially inflated view of us. If we derive a secret pleasure from being on a pedestal someone else has created for us, we could be setting ourselves up for a long, hard fall.

Equanimity reminds me of my inherent divinity and, likewise, the divinity of my sister and my brother.

There is danger in thinking that we are better than someone else, for whatever reason. There is also a danger in being gleeful (however secretly) about someone else's idea that we may be somehow better. Underpinning any idea that we are "better than" is a deep-rooted belief that we are somehow "less than."

There is also a danger in thinking we are worse than anyone else, which is the opposite side of the same coin of self-importance. When we believe everyone else is better than we are (or that there may be some people who are better than we are), it causes us to discount our gifts and talents from

God and not stand in the full radiance of who we are. This is pride in the reverse, which isn't humility. It is false pride. It's the idea of pretending to be insignificant, which may be used as a ploy to garner the comments of others who will insist that we are capable and worthy. If we need to hear from other people that we're capable and worthy in order for us to feel good, there is a field of misunderstanding within that must be examined and released. We must go within and find the roots of our gnawing need for external approval and uproot those tendencies. Remember:

You are God's idea of who you are.

With the principle of the eight winds, or, in one word, equanimity, we do not fall into the trap of putting others on a pedestal, nor do we secretly harbor ideas that we are better than anyone else. We remember God's implicit, unconditional love for each of us as an aspect of the One Life, which informs us that we are each blessed and divine beings of light, children of the Most High; each on our own journey of discovery.

Remember, you are God's idea of who you are.

Thoughts for Today

I am God's beloved child, on my own journey of self-discovery.

There is no order of importance and value among humans.

My value is intrinsic, built in when God made me.

I remain God-centered in the face of both lavish praise and stinging criticism.

There is no need for me to live up to what others have defined for me.

My mind stays centered on Spirit; my heart stays centered on peace.

I am God's idea of who I am.

Opposition

"In the world you have tribulation and trials and distress and frustration; but be of good cheer [take courage; be confident, certain, un-daunted]! For I have overcome the world. [I have deprived it of power to harm you and have conquered it for you.]"
John 16:33 (AMP)

"In the external universe there is ceaseless turmoil, change and unrest; at the heart of all things there is undisturbed repose; in this silence dwelleth the Eternal."
James Allen, *The Way of Peace*

There's a voice I hear internally that's never spoken more than four words at a time. Though it's required practice, I've grown to trust the voice, as it always adds something wise and knowing to my world.

"Opposition is your friend" is what it said to me one morning after an unsettling night.

I was going through a particularly tough time when the message came. I was deeply engaging myself in a mental battle over whether I should stay in my marriage or not. I say that I was engaged in a mental battle because it was all going on in my head. My spirit had spoken. It had said, quietly, calmly, and with total absence of malice or discontent: "Go within."

Well, when one lives in a beautiful home, with kids, and shared stuff, it's not easy to just pick up and go. Much more difficult, for me, was the feeling that I would have to explain what I was doing and why. Yes, we had been experiencing a fork-in-the-road feeling that was pulling us apart. Not so much disagreement as two ships going in different directions. Not so much the feeling of hurt as it was the feeling that it was just time to move on. The mind is a powerfully creative force, so I began to manufacture problems that would make it okay or at least acceptable for me to leave without having to explain.

The first problem here is that I didn't need to explain anything. Any attempt to explain what I want or what I'm feeling always gets me into trouble. It's not like the other person is going to understand, even after the explanation. Some things just have to be done; whether people understand them or not. Of course, in committed relationships, including marriage, there exists a responsibility to one's mate to share openly and honestly. If either party feels there needs to be a change in the commitment, full communication is in order.

In my relationship, we had been traveling on two different paths for quite a while, neither of us willing to truly acknowledge the extent of the drifting, and neither of us truly willing to bridge the gap. This kind of drift must be addressed and mended to have a healthy partnership.

I am a proponent of marriage and I believe in the deep level of commitment that must exist to make it meaningful and fulfilling. What I know about my marriage is that it had been inauthentic and riddled with lies. I wasn't genuinely myself. If I do not honor myself by living authentically, how can I tell a mate what I want or how to treat me? How can my mate respond? What would he respond to, the real me, whom he may only see on occasion, or the inauthentic version? It becomes too confusing.

One day, my husband said to me, "You're not the same person you were when we met. You don't know who you are." I found the comment interesting. The first part of the observation was accurate: I wasn't who I was when we first met eleven years prior. The second part of the observation I was in disagreement with, as I know now who I am more than ever: a divine child of God, infinitely loved and lovable. As far as roles were concerned, those had become quite muddled and confusing, so I guess the second part of the statement was factual as well, from his standpoint.

The question I next posed to my mate, after acknowledging his observations, was this: did I really change, or did the false me fall away only to reveal who I truly am?

I knew the answer before I asked the question: the false me had fallen away over time, only to reveal my true identity. And the kicker is that I knew my true identity all along; I was just too scared to embody it and live it lustily without apology.

A good friend of mine gave me profound feedback on what she observed in my marital relationship. I treasure her input. We were discussing the situation and she said that I appeared to be my authentic self in my other relationships, and people knew who I was and what I was about. However, she said I didn't seem to be my real self in my marriage. She said that other people knew who I was, but my husband didn't. I was being one way with some people, and another way at home.

That observation was so telling, I felt it in my gut. I did indeed have many faces. Many of us do, as a matter of social adjustment. However, my case went deeper than that. It was a case of depressing the real me for the comfort of someone else. I now view it as unacceptable behavior. And I knew that if I did this within the relationship, my inner guidance was telling me that I needed to be alone to explore my motives and reasons for giving away parts of myself. Why would I be willing to do that? What was the cost? What was the payoff? What would it mean for me long-term and for the relationship? How would it impact my children?

There were so many questions, they deserved to be explored and answered.

What I knew about myself was that I'd created a false identity to do the impossible: keep my mate happy, safe, and feeling comfortable. *Don't rock the boat. Don't make waves.*

The problem with that line of thinking is sometimes the boat needs rocking. Sometimes the best thing that can be done is to make waves.

Living without authenticity is tiring—it's wearying to wear a false face. What I also knew was that my pseudoself's days were numbered. She

had to go. She was causing way too much trouble
with way too little payoff. The false identity began to fall away once it become too painful and
tiring to live a lie, or more accurately, a pack of
lies. I was unhappy with myself. I wasn't able to
look myself in the eye and smile; I knew I had betrayed myself and my desires on too many occasions and was apt to do it again if circumstances
were ripe.

Somewhere along the way, and I can't say
exactly when it happened, or even if it happened
all at once, I made a monumental decision to
relinquish the mask and be authentic, no matter
what. No matter what people think, no matter
who says what, no matter what the rules are.
Just be authentic, Valerie. Just be who you truly
are, without reservation, hesitation, procrastination, explanation, or justification. Just be who
you truly are. Live authentically.

When one makes a radical decision, the earth
shakes. What I thought to be the firm ground I
had planted my life on began to rock and rumble.
No longer was I standing. My whole life seemed
to wobble. I'd never imagined that such a self-
supportive decision would rock everything in my
world to its very foundation. I'd never imagined
that so much turmoil would come out of such a
positive stance.

The reason there was so much turmoil, I suspect, is because my entire life was set up around the false persona, not the real me. When the false face eroded, everything attached to it began to erode and fall away, too—friends, family members, religion, business endeavors, and inauthentic relationships. All of it fell away in the rumble. I stood there, looking at the heap and rejoicing over its beauty. It's beautiful to stand in my true identity as a divine being and lovingly look at all that has fallen away and to be able to rejoice over it.

I changed religions. As it turned out, the religion in which I'd been reared and associated with for over thirty years of my life turned out not to be for me at all. It was the furthest thing from my true identity, purpose, and calling.

I ended my first marriage. I now see the relationship as a blessed learning experience.

I sold my business. I left my financial planning practice to live my dreams and passions. The decision sprung from an inner commitment and determination to live on purpose. I chose to teach and write books about what really matters to me: growth and transformation.

In the midst of it all, there is perfect peace. It all works together for my good. I feel like a new being, a new creation; not new in the sense that it didn't exist before, it's new in the sense that I am now living authentically. It is a fairly new behavior for me.

In retrospect, the false persona provided just the resistance and opposition I needed to make a change. When I felt the resistance or opposition, I knew something was askew and needed to be addressed. It was usually a question of me not doing something that truly fulfilled me while kowtowing to someone else's needs or wants.

One example I recall is my current husband desiring a mate who would cook and be the domestic maven his mom is. I've never been a domestic maven, not even close. Nor do I have the remotest desire to be. From the day we met, we went out to dinner on most dates. I don't remember even one occasion where I invited him over for a meal I'd prepared. It just wasn't me. I hate cooking. I hate grocery shopping. I only do it out of necessity or I pay someone to do it for me. So for me to even remotely think that I could be a housewife who cooks dinners, even if not every night, was an abject lie to myself and the people I love. When I did stand at the stove and cook, I could feel the conflict within me, sometimes to a greater degree, sometimes to a lesser degree, but always present because I wasn't doing what genuinely bought me joy. Even worse, it was an activity I actually disdained. I stood over the food thinking of all the things I'd rather be doing than standing in the kitchen. It's little wonder the food I cooked wasn't delicious; it was infused with negative energy.

Had I been authentic about this matter, I would have stated, before getting married, "Honey, let's be real. You've known me for eight years and the number of dinners I've cooked for you can be counted on one-and-a-half hands. When we get married, I will not be the chef of the family. I don't enjoy cooking, nor do I enjoy grocery shopping—I actually think I'm allergic to both activities. Since you love to cook and you get a thrill out of it, would you like to take on that role, and I will always clean up the kitchen after meals?" This is just one possible solution out of countless solutions. Either way, I stay true to myself. Rather than promising to be in the kitchen making meals and playing the role of Good Little Miss Housewife, I tell the truth and say I haven't played house before and I'm not about to start. Then, I ask my mate squarely, "Can you live with that?" If he can't live with it, it's okay. At least I've spoken my honest truth and there are no inauthentic expectations going into a marriage. Expectations based upon assumptions, lies, and pretenses breed contempt because they will, most assuredly, be dashed. This is a minor example of inauthentic living, yet it has far-reaching implications. If I do not live authentically in the small things, what else will I lie about?

If I don't know who I am, or if I choose to live inauthentically, I open the door for people to come along who are only too happy to offer their ideas on how my life should be lived. Everyone else will offer their ideas on how my life should be lived, as I've not taken a stand to live my life the way I know it can be lived.

Now that I know who I am, and have made the conscious choice to live authentically, I've opened another door in my life, one for folks who will support me in being authentic. They are not threatened by my truth. The reason my truth doesn't threaten them is because they're living their truth. An authentic human being is never afraid of another authentic human being. On the flip side, an inauthentic person will be intimidated by, if not frightened to near death of, a truly authentic person, especially if she's not ready to relinquish the false mask. And as for an inauthentic person and another inauthentic person, they may party together for a period, until one of them gets tired and wants out, or until both come to the realization and work toward full authenticity together.

Either way, each person's journey is perfect for them.

Yes, the voice was right. Opposition is my friend. I've run into much of it, building muscles galore.

God loves us unconditionally and will always allow us free reign to create our own resistance and opposition if that's the way we choose to build muscle, though it isn't a necessary learning path for an expanded and authentic life. It can be easier.

Live well and true to you.

Thoughts for Today

I know who I am: I am divine and very holy.

I live my truth and invite others to do the same.

I love being me!

There's no one else I'd rather be!

I am perfect, just the way God made me.

I am unique and I live my most authentic life.

My true identity needs no explanation.

Opposition is my friend.

I have strong muscles.

When I am true to myself, I am true to God.

Truth

"And you will know the Truth, and the Truth
will set you free."
John 8:32 (AMP)

"Everything comes out in the wash."
Jacqueline McIntosh (my mom)

I had just found out I had been in an adulterous marriage.

I had a conversation with one of my close girlfriends about it. In the conversation, I shared with her what my mate had shared with me about an incident that had occurred.

"He told me he stepped outside our marriage," I said.

"He what?" was her response.

"You heard correctly. He admitted to me the other day that he had stepped outside our marriage."

"Well, I could understand the other stuff you two had going on, but this makes me mad!"

I didn't have the same reaction. I knew. We always know. We always know when someone we're in close relationship with is not completely committed to the relationship. For me, it meant on some level that I, myself, was not fully committed to the relationship.

I wasn't surprised at the news because there had been a growing distance between us. Distance invites partners to stray. When it happens, there's no need to blame. It's simply time for examination. What is the distance I'm feeling within that causes me to distance myself from my mate? What am I not able to talk about that causes a divide? What am I holding back? What am I not saying? How am I not being the real me?

Truth is like a dead body that's been thrown into the ocean. The ocean doesn't accept dead bodies—she always sends them back. I'm not sure why people keep trying to dispose of dead bodies in the ocean when they always wash ashore. They come home to roost and tell their horrid stories.

The same happens with truth. A loving life does not abide falsehoods. Sooner or later, one way or the other, the whole truth will come floating back to shore. It may stink to high heaven, and it may look quite ugly, but there it is. When it comes ashore, it must be handled. Just like a dead body.

This bit of truth from my mate about the adultery was a dead body experience for me. The news came floating ashore unannounced, unexpected, and unwelcome.

Part of me wanted to get mad. Part of me wanted to say, "I knew it." Part of me wanted to call him a pig and act like a victim. Part of me wanted to know why he was talking about this now, considering that we were, at that time, separated and living in two different households. None of these voices was the authentic me.

The real me—the authentic me—was calm and unaffected. The calm part of me surprised the other parts of me. Being calm in the midst of a situation like this one was new for me. If this dead body had washed ashore just a year earlier, I would've had an openly adverse reaction. I would've thrown a fit right there on the beach with my hair standing on end, yelling and screaming "how could you do this to me!" I had a penchant for dropping into victim behavior. This would have been an opportunity for me to see just how far into being a victim I could sink.

That was then. This is now.

In this most recent conversation, there was no adverse reaction. Just an "Oh." The relief he felt in telling me was palpable, so I chalked up the conversation to his need to express, confess, and hopefully feel better.

Innately, I knew the act had nothing to do with me, while it concurrently had everything to do with me.

First, it had nothing to do with me because everyone makes their own choices. I am responsible for my choices and my choices only. I am not responsible for anyone else, even if the person shares my genes or my last name; this holds true particularly if they share my genes and last name. I am learning not to take what other people do personally by staying out of the kitchen. What that means is I have had the habit of going into the kitchen of my life's experiences and cooking up stories about what things mean. I could have cooked up quite a story in this situation about what the whole thing meant. When I let myself go, and forget my true spiritual identity, I begin to think stray thoughts about what things must mean. What things mean, in my cooked up stories, doesn't coincide with divine truth.

Cooked up story: I must not be desirable; that's what this must mean.

Truth: I am desirable. I am lovable, and I love me from the inside out.

Cooked up story: I must not be worthy of having someone who will love me and only me.

Truth: God is in love with me and that's all I'll ever need. Since I know from God's love that I am unconditionally lovable, I love me unconditionally.

Cooked up story: There must be something wrong with me.

Truth: I am perfect, whole, and complete, just as I am.

Cooked up story: Maybe the other woman is more beautiful than me. Maybe she has something I don't have. Maybe she can rock his world in bed better than I can. Yeah, maybe that's it.

Truth: I compare myself to the most excellent and magnificent version of who I could be; that is the only comparison I engage in. I place my focus on all I could be and work toward that end. When God made me, the mold was broken!

When we erroneously determine what things mean, the story usually isn't true. In addition, faulty thought leads to faulty feelings, which lead to faulty actions.

Faulty Actions: Just who is this other woman anyway? I wonder what she looks like and where she works. After all, I just might show up at her job one day and curse her out and tell her to keep her grubby paws off my man or I'll kick her tail. Yeah, that's what I'll do.

It's clear that determining what things mean can land us in serious trouble. It is never beneficial to interpret what someone says or does, and then use the interpretation to define who we are, or allow it to define even an aspect of who we are. Other people's actions, in truth, do not define us, even when we decide that they do.

Nothing anyone does has anything to do with you. What others do only has to do with what's going on inside of them. When you know this all the way to your core, the discovery engenders transformation.

Concurrently, the adulterous acts had everything to do with me. I say this because one of my most present innermost fears in my marriage was adultery. I had already had the experience of being in a committed relationship and my mate having a tryst. I had also been at the other end of the spectrum; I had stepped out of my previous marriage and had a tryst. So the whole tryst idea was burned into my psyche. My faulty thinking was: *Adultery and fooling around goes along with the territory of being married or in a committed relationship. People cheat. Sooner or later, someone's going to stray. And that's just the way things are.*

Yet deep inside, despite my faulty thinking, my heart desired a true heart connection in a partner, one in which both of us thrived mentally, emotionally, spiritually, and physically. I knew adultery, in any form—mental, emotional, or physical—was not what I desired for myself. So I decided to dig deeper into my thought process. While I recognize his act as having nothing to do with me and having to do only with what was going on inside of him at the time, I must take responsibility for my contribution to the act because the act is in my world, and everything in my world is here by my creation or by my invitation. Nothing—no person, situation, or issue—can come into my world unless and only if I allow it, invite it, or create it myself. I examined myself for the reasons I would create and/or invite this situation into my world. What was I ready to learn now?

The answers became abundantly clear, as always occurs when we have the courage to start asking questions, especially of ourselves.

Lurking just beneath the surface of my faulty thinking was a destructive and debilitating fear: *inevitably someone is going to hurt me by cheating on me. They will leave, or I will leave and then I'll be alone.* I discovered an unaddressed fear of abandonment.

I was in this situation and relationship because of my faulty thinking and the fear I emanated. It's almost as if my fears were a huge magnet attracting people who would most surely do the very things I feared most.

This organic and natural process unfolds so we can eliminate fears and live courageously, which is God's idea for us. What we usually end up doing is getting mad at the person who outwardly embodies our internal fears.

The root cause of the trysts in my life—whether I was engaged in one myself or in a relationship with someone who was engaged in one—was my internal fear of abandonment. Not wanting to be alone, or left, was a very real fear. Fear is a powerful motivator. This deep fear caused me to engage myself in situations and circumstances that externalized it and literally gave it legs.

This whole wonderful process of self-discovery, for me, was so beautiful. How would I really know what was going on within me without the benefit of these external embodiments in the form of lovers and mates?

God showed me my fears up close and personal. Only then could I deal with each one. Only then could I apply God's love to my dreads and tell each one *all is well*. Only then could I take full responsibility for my relationships. The fears are still present and, at times, very vocal. However, now that they've been discovered, they're no longer allowed to drive me or my behaviors in relationships.

Once an internal fear is unmasked, it loses power.

The truth is not always easy, just like a dead body. Yet, the truth is vital, for the process of healing and growth can't unfold without it.

I will not grow and heal from this relationship unless I look at it in all its dysfunction. I consciously choose to look at what I created, so I can wisely choose to create differently going forward. It's all a blessing. All things work together for my good, and the perfect learning opportunity is present in every situation. I simply need to stay open and aware.

On occasion, my learning comes in the form of a dead body: quite unexpected and quite unpleasant.

Despite the distastefulness of what I was hearing from my mate, I found a space of perfect peace in that conversation. I was in no position to judge, having done the same thing previously. So I sat quietly, listening, and assimilating what was being said. I stood on the beach, watching the dead body slowly roll over waves to wash gently ashore and land at my feet.

Truth always surfaces, proof positive of God's unconditional love at work. You can handle any truth if you make room for the love.

When you have a dead body experience, stand in peace on the beach, knowing, with full trust, that everything works together for your good.

God's love is the insurance policy on dead bodies.

Thoughts for Today

Truth always surfaces and it sets me free.

I can handle any truth with a soul full of love.

All things work together for my good, and everything works out perfectly according to divine will.

I lovingly look at my creations and re-create as I desire.

Self-discovery is beautiful and miraculous—it is why I am here.

I find perfect peace in every dead body experience.

I am continually learning.

My life gets better and better with each new choice.

Well-being

"I have no enemies, and all is well."
1 Kings 5:4 (NLT)

"There is no arbitrary power in the universe,
and the strongest chains of fate by which men
are bound are self-forged."
James Allen, *The Way of Peace*

Albert Einstein stated that the most important question we must ask ourselves is: do I live in a friendly universe?

When I first heard his statement, I had little intellectual grasp of all it implied, yet it resonated with me. I had no idea, at the time, of how pivotal the act of making this decision would be for me and what it would mean for my future. Years passed before I came to understand the question's poignancy and its relevance to everything I do.

Before I share with you how this issue has un-folded for me, let's explore the question a little further.

Einstein's query is one that demands our at-tention: is this a friendly universe?

The question is profound because your answer to it colors everything about how you perceive the world around you. If you believe this to be a friendly universe, your over-arching view of life is one of feeling supported and befriended. If you believe this to be an unfriendly universe, your life experiences will reflect your feelings of victimization.

Either way, it's your choice. How you choose to see your world has everything to do with how you will experience your world. There are no ex-ceptions. Your thoughts, perceptions, and beliefs create and color your entire existence. Do you hold the life belief that you reside in a friendly universe? Or, do you hold a life belief that hints of conspiracy theories and paranoia? Your world will be created and colored with whatever life beliefs you hold as truth.

The good news is: you get to choose your be-liefs; you and only you.

The not-so-good news is: your beliefs are just that, your beliefs. They may or may not be the truth, though they play out to be true for you. They may or may not be sensible. They are simply your beliefs. And as such, they deserve to be challenged. Every belief you've ever held deserves to be challenged, for your own good.

I did it, not so much because I wanted to. It was more because my soul set it up in such a way that examining my every belief became a requisite for my continued growth and freedom. I came to see the wisdom in the practice of challenging every belief I hold in consciousness, whether known or unknown.

As I began to take on my beliefs, one by one (and sometimes by the handful or by the dozen), I made an important and somewhat disturbing discovery. Most of the beliefs I had held in consciousness as truth actually had been handed to me from what seems like an endless array of individuals, tribes, and groups. There were the beliefs of my father and mother, the beliefs of their parents, the beliefs of the religious organization to which we were linked, the beliefs of my teachers and school administrators, the beliefs of my friends, the beliefs of the social organizations with which I interacted, the beliefs within my cultural code, and several sundry and varied beliefs that I actually have no idea where they came from.

In the process of growing to physical maturity, beliefs come at us from an array of sources. Considering the source of most of our beliefs makes them suspect. I mean, would you accept just anything anyone gave you? You'd probably have some questions. And, if you're like me, you had lots of questions about the beliefs you were given as you were growing up. And, like me, you may have been told: "That's just the way it is," or "Don't ask so many questions," or "Don't question God," or "Do as I say," or whatever else the party who was handing out beliefs that day decided to tell you.

I've made a life choice to endeavor, to stand, and to walk in truth. Before I can walk in truth, I've got to return to the truth as it is revealed to me by God. The way I return to the truth is to create a space within me for the truth to stand. That happens through my readiness and willingness to question and challenge everything I think I already know, namely, everything I believe. When I stand willing and ready to release what I think I know (through my voluntary scrutiny of all I hold as true) in favor and expectancy of something new, the truth springs up spontaneously.

What is truth? Good question. It's an old question, too.

Truth is immutable, unchangeable, and inde-structible. Truth doesn't change with the weather; it is eternally changeless. This way of describing truth sounds somewhat esoteric, yet truth has a quality of being grounded and stable. Truth is most times astonishingly simple and almost always easily digestible and understandable. Truth has a distinctive ring; when we hear it, we know it.

Truth is a measuring stick for life. Folks are only too ready to hand us their beliefs as if they were absolute truth. To guard against falling into the trap of taking other people's beliefs as the gospel truth, we can weigh the new information—or the old information—against a universal truth to see how it measures up. If what we are being presented with, or have been presented with, doesn't measure up to the universal truth, we know what to do with the information: put it in the file of interesting information, not the file of absolute truth. A universal truth is: God is love. This we know as truth and we can measure our beliefs against this timeless, changeless principle. I've measured all my beliefs against this universal truth and have had to release countless ideas that didn't match it.

How is truth revealed? Good question. God reveals truth and it resides in all spiritual traditions, so it cannot be claimed as the exclusive possession or domain of any one sect or group. Truth is revealed by God to any and every person who asks.

How do we ask? Good question. We ask by sitting in the silence, being still and quiet, simply being. You could call it meditation, reflection, or contemplation. What we call it makes no difference. The powerful spiritual practice of being still, quiet, and open to God's revelation is what we're going for here. The more time you spend quietly "being," the more truth will be revealed. I know this sounds quite simple, yet simplicity is the nature of truth.

So it would follow that the path to truth is equally as simple: sit down and shut up.

I've often gone into a meditative or reflective period with a question in mind. It may be a simple question, or it could be a complex life issue I've been grappling with. When I sit down, silently ask my question, and remain quiet, open, and receptive to whatever unfolds, I receive answers. Truth is revealed. It's not something we have to go in search of. The doorway to truth is ever-present within each of us. You don't have to go on a quest. All you need do is sit quietly with the awareness and understanding that truth is spontaneously revealed in the perfect unfolding of divine will and timing. This approach to revelation demands patience. All the mysteries of the Universe won't be revealed to you in five minutes of sitting still. Yet, if you're willing to develop a spiritual practice of sitting in stillness each day, you'll begin to receive revelation after revelation. Truth will surface from deep within your very being.

There are two kinds of truth that may surface for you. The aforementioned universal truth is all-encompassing, eternal, and changeless. As mentioned, an example of a universal truth is: God is love. Universal truth transcends race, culture, tribal customs, religion, creed, social class, country, and gender. Another universal truth is that love is attractive. No matter who you are, or where you live, or who raised you, you are attracted to love. Love is one of the most irresistible forces in the Universe. Such universal truths apply to every person who inhabits the cosmos. Universal truth is spontaneously and continuously revealed to us in our practice of silent meditation.

Another kind of truth, also revealed in silence, is personal truth. Personal truth is individualized and custom-made for each of us. What may be personal truth for me may not be personal truth for you. I find that this is where we, as

members of the human race, get ourselves into
more trouble than a little. We hold a belief that
has proven to be personal truth for us, and then
we tend to propagate and promote it to our
brothers and sisters as universal truth.

Before expounding on this concept, now would
be an appropriate time to address and clarify the
differences among a belief, personal truth, and
universal truth.

A belief is a thought you've entertained repeatedly, have held for a long time, and have
energized and infused with emotion. You feel
passionately about your beliefs. You've held onto
a thought for so long, and with such emotion,
that the thought has become amplified. Once a
thought turns into a belief, it has great creative
and magnetic power. Your beliefs are creating
your world.

Beliefs are tricky because they become self-
fulfilling prophecies, which causes us to hold on
to them even more fervently. Since our beliefs
manifest themselves and become our entire
life experience, they tend to grow stronger and
more deeply entrenched. If you believe people
are stupid, you'll meet up with lots of people
who appear to be stupid to you. This will only
solidify your belief that people are stupid. If you
believe all people are naturally good at the core,

you'll meet up with people who seem to be good-natured. Your belief in the inherent good nature of people will continue to deepen and solidify through your life experience. Either way, when you meet up with experience after experience that agrees with whatever you believe, you adopt a "see, I told you so" view of the world.

The double-edged sword is that you are creating and attracting the experiences of your life through the power of your beliefs. Your life experience doesn't prove your beliefs true or right, though we tend to argue that it does. Your experience just proves that whatever you believe will manifest. Change your beliefs and your life experience will change accordingly. This is the major reason why all beliefs must be challenged. You don't know if your beliefs are truth, or if they're just playing out in certain patterns because you believe that's the way things are.

Some of our beliefs are not even in our conscious awareness; they're insidiously creating negative results without us being consciously aware of it. The first step in releasing beliefs that are personally destructive and debilitating is to become aware of their presence. One of the most effective means by which to uncover beliefs of all kinds is through the practice of meditation. Once we become aware of the presence of negative beliefs, we can choose to allow them to be dislodged from our consciousness and released. For this, we have access to the Holy Spirit, which works within us to heal and restore our minds to holiness, which is wholeness. We're able to clearly see our beliefs and what type of outcomes they're creating when we expose them to the light of God's holy spirit.

Beliefs can be turned into personal truth, but not always. While beliefs can either be destructive or constructive, debilitating or empowering, personal truth is always empowering, rewarding, supportive, and loving for the person who holds such truth. Personal truth, in the context we are discussing here, is never personally destructive or debilitating. It is the stabilizing influence in life that keeps us grounded in the face of life's storms and changes. Personal truth is like a great boulder in the middle of a raging ocean. It's what sustains us in spiritual practice and in life. It is always personally liberating and uplifting. It is the path which leads to freedom and love.

How do we arrive at personal truth? How do we take our beliefs from simply being something we've thought about for a long time and infused with a fair amount of emotion, into a self-liberating and self-supportive personal truth? Once again, the answer awaits us in the silence. When we're silent, prayerful, and contemplative, we discover much about our beliefs. We discover which beliefs can be elevated to the level of personal truth and which beliefs can be discarded. This is a living-from-within approach rather than the popular "getting your beliefs from the outside" approach.

Let's go back to the earlier example of the "people are stupid" belief. No matter how much you meditate upon it, this belief simply does not have the power to be raised from the level of a belief to the level of personal truth because it contains inherently flawed thinking. Further, it's a personally destructive thought and it's destructive to others. It doesn't agree with the nature of the cosmos; God didn't create humans to be stupid. Though people may act stupid on occasion, some on more occasions than others, no one is stupid all the time. No one was created stupid. While this belief may bring its bearer into contact with people who are having stupid moments, this thought cannot be sustained nor can it be proven true.

Let's look back at the example of the "people are good-natured" belief. This belief does have the power and ability to be expanded and advanced to the level of personal truth, because God did make us to be good, and declared us so after creation. Even under the most dastardly deeds, there is a heart. The belief that people are inherently good is a liberating and loving thought, both for the person who holds this belief and for all parties involved. Living life according to this standard brings only benefits. This belief can indeed be advanced to the level of personal truth. The personal truth that people are good-natured can even be heightened to the level of universal truth because we are each and all made in the image of the One who created us. We are made of the same stuff as our Creator. We are each and all naturally good. This is an example of a belief that can be proven to be a liberating and supportive personal truth as well as a universal truth.

One way to see our beliefs for what they truly are is through prayer and silent reflection. Once we see a belief for what it truly is, either destructive or personal truth, we have a choice. We can discard the beliefs that have been revealed as unloving and non-supportive fallacies, or we can choose not to. We always have choices. Just because you discover that one or many of your beliefs are creating negative outcomes doesn't mean that you have to, or will, automatically eliminate it. The difference is that the awareness is now present to make better and more appropriate choices. Before you know what your beliefs are, you have no awareness; therefore, you'll be challenged in making appropriate choices. Awareness leads to actualizing your power of choice.

Personal truth is revealed, once again, in silent, meditative states.

I mentioned earlier that personal truth is never personally destructive, in and of itself. However, if used in unloving ways, a personal truth can be turned into a weapon. This occurs when we attempt to force or coerce others into accepting and/or adopting our personal truth as universal truth, when, in actuality, it isn't. Wars are waged when holders of a particular set of personal truths attempt to forcefully convince others that these personal truths are universal truths, when they aren't.

Here's an example of how this happens, and how we get into disputes and divides over personal truth:

I was teaching one of my workshops when I came to the part where we examine and challenge beliefs. I was speaking to a group of women in America, many of whom were Christian. When I gave an example of one of the beliefs that should be challenged, the energy in the room shifted.

What I said, in essence, was, "An example of a belief to be challenged is that Jesus Christ is Lord and Savior."

I heard gasps in the room. Some of the women stared at me, as if to brace themselves for where I was going with the idea. I paused for a moment to allow the idea to sink in.

Jesus Christ is Lord and Savior is a deeply held belief by millions of people. For many of those millions, it is also personal truth. For those who have found this to be a personal truth, it is because they have discovered, through their own spiritual practice, that Jesus Christ is truly their Lord and Savior. It is no longer a belief that has been handed to them by parents, culture, or society, but has been elevated to the level of personal truth in their lives through direct spiritual experience and revelation. This personal truth becomes liberating, supportive, and empowering for those who hold it.

Yet, this personal truth is not universal truth. It is not the truth for all humans everywhere. Countless wars have been fought between people who hold the personal truth that Jesus Christ is Lord and Savior and those who do not. In this case, to believe that Jesus Christ is Lord and Savior is supportive for the person who holds this personal truth. Whether it is personal truth for each of us is, once again, revealed in the silence of contemplation. Go into the silence and ask who Christ is to you. If you're willing and dare to ask the question, truth will be revealed; both personal truth and universal truth with regard to Jesus Christ and his role in your life. You may have been told that He is your Lord and Savior. Yet is He?

I choose not to accept as truth, either personal or universal, what someone else tells me about Jesus Christ. I don't assume that He must be my personal Lord and Savior just because the people who told me about Him (such as parents, teachers, friends, and religious leaders) knew Him to be their personal Lord and Savior. As I developed my spiritual practice of going into the silence and simply asking, it became clearer and clearer to me over time who Christ is to me personally. His role continues to be expanded, clarified, and intensified in my experience. I've come to see things from a different vantage point. After challenging this personally held and widely held belief, I came to my own personal satisfying truth about Jesus Christ and who He is to me. It's been a beautiful unfolding revelation. If I had simply accepted what people told me about Jesus Christ, I may have never asked the questions I did. The answers have led to an illustrious understanding of who Jesus Christ is to me. It turns out that the Jesus Christ people told me about and the Jesus Christ I've come to know in my own spiritual journey of awakening are two very different entities.

It takes a deep level of courage and an outrageous willingness to ask these kinds of questions, because the answers can be life-changing. On a scale of all the unsettling things in the world, finding out that you had a faulty belief system, though you were convinced it was right, ranks quite high. The discovery can be painful. Yet, in order for both personal and universal truth to be revealed, the questions must be asked. And they must be asked of every belief; no belief is too holy or sacred to be challenged.

My personal truth does not equate to universal truth. And I'm okay with that discovery. I wasn't at first. I wanted to believe that what I held as personal truth was true for everyone, everywhere, all the time. I even used to knock on doors and proselytize that this was the case. I tried to convince people to adopt my personal truth as theirs. It didn't work, for me or for them.

Now I know the differences among my beliefs, my personal truths, and universal truth. I love Jesus Christ and I know there are many who do not, and that is as it should be. God made a flower garden, and in that stunning array of diverse beauty, the rose doesn't taunt the carnation. We must not allow ourselves to become embroiled in taunting our brother and sister, regardless of race, religion, gender, sexual persuasion, age, social class/status, employment, or any other limiting and separating manner we have for carving up the world into billions of tiny little pieces. There is only God's stunning and diverse flower garden. And it is all good.

Great care must be exercised so that personal truth is not elevated to the level of universal truth in our minds, thus turning it into a weapon against our brother or sister. When we declare or assert that personal truth is universal truth, we are bound to create conflict and a lose-lose proposition, which only invites disagreement, discord, and disharmony. My personal truth is just that, my personal truth, which is designed to support me in navigating life's ups and downs. I do not have the right to declare my personal truth to be the universal truth for everyone, everywhere, all the time.

Never be afraid to question your deeply held beliefs. Never be afraid to rigorously examine all you thought of as truth. The truth, both personal and universal, can stand up to tough scrutiny. The rest of the stuff that was handed to us will crumble and fall under the heat of serious and soulful investigation.

Scrutinizing my belief system revealed a wide chasm between the beliefs I hold now and the beliefs I was handed as a young person. The chasm first appeared when I discovered that a great many of my beliefs had a weakening influence, while some were downright destructive.

When we topple a major belief, most of the smaller ones that were propped up against it automatically fall. So I encourage you to go for the gusto in this process. Go for challenging your most deeply entrenched, passionately held beliefs first. There's a big payoff in taking this approach. Going for the big beliefs is more about making a bold statement to your inner being— and to the Universe—that there's nothing you hold more sacred than knowing and being the truth. When you look at your biggest beliefs— your inner giants—you'll see what's running the show called your life. Your biggest beliefs are creating everything in your world. They're running your entire life.

When you challenge these inner Goliaths, you make a bold move to take back one of your most potent powers: *your power to choose*. God's love ensures you always have the right and the power to choose. And choose again. And choose again. And to keep choosing until you get it the way you want it.

When you hold a belief that's strongly entrenched, it diminishes your power to choose. Why? Because you're no longer the one doing the choosing; your beliefs are doing the choosing for you.

Let's examine this point using a giant among beliefs: religious persuasion. Most people practice the religion of their parents, which is suspect in and of itself. Going further, whatever your religion is (and it doesn't matter what your religion is for the purposes of this discussion), your religion is probably making a lot of choices for you, including and certainly not limited to: where and what you eat, how you pray, where and how you worship, where and how you engage in recreation and social interaction. Depending upon how strictly you adhere to your religion, it could be the entire context and framework from which you operate.

In accepting the religion of your parents, you've accepted a packaged belief system. And maybe, just maybe, some of what's in that package that was handed to you is not congruent with your authentic self. And maybe, just maybe, you may not always feel fully aligned with what you practice as a religious tradition.

If you feel an inkling or have even a vague idea of what I'm talking about here, it may be time for you to challenge your religious belief system. Go ahead, you're grown. You have permission. After all, you're the boss of what goes on inside you, not your parents, not your social circles, and not your minister. If what you're doing now is confirmed by your inner being, your sacred and most holy self, congratulations. You are on a path of spiritual discovery which satisfies your soul.

However, if what you're doing now raises questions within you, or causes you to want to search and seek, or if you're just curious, by all means, dive into the discovery of who you truly are. Ask the questions you've always wanted to ask. Perhaps you have never received an answer. As you ask these important questions of self-discovery, notice the thoughts and feelings that surface. The answers may be astounding. You may discover you're not really who you thought you were at all. How beautiful that would be.

The answer is not quite so important as how you feel within yourself when you ask the question. You may notice resistance rising, or you may feel righteously indignant. Just notice what happens within as you challenge your biggest beliefs.

I'll share with you the process of challenging one of the giant-sized beliefs I'd been carrying around for years as "the truth," which ties to our Einstein question at the outset.

The belief I carried about the nature of the Universe was slowly eroding my ability to become the person I desired to be: one who lives a life of purpose. Challenging the belief, for me, was a bold and courageous step in choosing to consciously design and create a life I love. Here's how the process unfolded.

As a young person, I was taught that there is an evil, organized influence who is roaming everywhere, seeking to devour me at any moment. This evil influence has my destruction and death in mind and is bent on making it happen as quickly as possible. The evil force was called Satan the Devil and was said to be like a roaring lion, ready to pounce upon me and strip me to smithereens. I was taught that there's a malicious, non-stop onslaught from this evil one directed at me and every human alive. The goal: to lure us away from God, and ultimately, to destroy us.

Considering Einstein's question, this belief didn't give me the feeling of living in a friendly universe. How could the Universe be friendly when there was a raging and destructive, hell-bent and evil force lurking everywhere who only wanted to kill me? How could the Universe be friendly when there's evil blocking and resisting me at every turn? *No*, I thought to myself, *this is definitely not a friendly universe and I need to act accordingly.*

The people who taught me about this evil ever-present force called Satan the Devil didn't have ill intent when they handed me the doctrine; they thought they were helping me. I believe they were trying their best to protect me. However, what it conjured up in my mind were ideas of paranoia and evil conspiracy, and what it conjured up in my body were feelings of not being safe. While it's true I was simultaneously taught God is love and is always there to help me, that idea (in my young mind) didn't seem to have the same level of intensity accompanying it as the devil story. Somehow, the idea of the devil and his evil hordes of demons conjured up wild and destructive images in my mind, while the God-is-love idea couldn't always allay my fears.

While growing up, I remember Satan the Devil being a big-time enemy in our house. He got blamed for almost everything that went wrong. We had to be vigilant when it came to this character, including being watchful of people and what they gave us and items purchased second-hand from consignment shops and flea markets. I was taught that if we brought the wrong items into the house—perhaps from someone who'd had demon contact—the demons would then have a bridge to cross over to get into our home. Once the house was "demonized," there would be real problems. All manner of mischief and mayhem could be perpetrated upon the near helpless inhabitants of our home at the hands of the invisible demons, including items floating in midair, dead people sitting around in the living room, or objects being hurled across the room for no apparent reason and with no human intervention. This whole devil and demons story was quite frightening, and I remember frequently waking up at night in cold sweats, deathly afraid to move, imagination running wildly and conjuring up all sorts of disturbing images.

No, this was not the intent of the folks who perpetuated the story, I'm sure. Yet, to me, it was a frightening and debilitating story. This is not to say whether the story is true one way or the other. Some people believe in devils and demons and some do not. That is not the subject of this discussion. The subject of this discussion is how the story made me feel, and was it helpful or was it harmful? Was it a productive story, or was it debilitating?

I chose to begin the journey of asking these questions because I'd become aware of destructive patterns which were operating in my psyche and becoming manifest in my life. The patterns were held in place by beliefs which had become rooted in my consciousness, such as: there's always going to be resistance to whatever I want; there's an evil, intelligent, and organized force, which opposes me at every turn; I'll have to fight to get whatever I want and need; life is very, very hard and I may not survive the attacks that are surely being mounted against me each day. No! This is not a friendly universe!

None of these beliefs are the truth, though I succeeded in making them my reality. None of these beliefs are empowering. They're all limiting on some level, some of them playing out in destructively insidious ways. As my life unfolded, I began to see that my idea and thought of this being an unfriendly universe was causing me to conduct myself in ways that didn't get me positive results. Defensiveness, negativity, victim-hood, doubt, and fear were the negative by-products of the mentality I'd adopted. It was easy to blame all my woes on a hated outside entity that was bent on my destruction. It was the perfect alibi, socially acceptable and carrying the stamp of approval from religion.

There was a television show I enjoyed watching while growing up in the 1970s that featured the comedian Flip Wilson. He'd created an infamous character named Geraldine, a woman who, when caught red-handed in a mess of her own creation, would shout: "The devil made me do it!" I had my own internal version of Geraldine whenever I was caught red-handed in a mess of my own creation: *the devil is at work again. Look what he made me do this time.*

My persistent habit of using the devil as an alibi didn't seem to be working. The blame game I was playing was siphoning off my power. I didn't know how; I just instinctively felt it to be so.

It was high time for a change. So I examined this belief and challenged it. While I know that there is light and there is darkness, I also know that the darkness flees from the light. It's not the other way around. There is never a need for me to fear darkness, regardless of how frightening or terrifying it may seem. There is a need, however, if I am to be in perfect peace, to examine my inner world and allow God's love to shine light on my inner darkness. As I stand in the light of truth and consciously choose to allow God's love to flow through me into the world, I am fully protected in all I am and all I do.

There was one more thing. I couldn't reconcile my belief system of a negative intelligent force with something I knew in my core to be true: God is omnipotent (all powerful), omnipresent (everywhere present), and omniscient (all knowing). I questioned the belief that there was an intelligent, organized opposing force outside of me that was capable of blocking me, resisting me, keeping me from my good, and causing me to perform all manner of personally destructive acts. Darkness flees from the light, this I know.

Could I believe that there was a default position that we, as humans, can decay to if we do not take forward holy action? Yes. Could I believe that there was an inner enemy who would cause mayhem and mischief in my world if left unchecked? Yes. Could I believe that what unfolds in my world is my responsibility, not to be blamed on an outside devil? Yes.

It is enlightening that the mystical tradition of Kaballah speaks of Satan as being a code word for chaos. In the Hebrew language, the word Satan (pronounced Su-tahn) is a code word for the chaos that completely rules the physical world of effects, in which we interact with our five senses. Functioning only at the physical sense level, without conscious connection to the spirit realms, is chaotic. Our senses lie. They tell us things are one way when they're not that way at all. We don't see things as they are; we see them as we are. Our perceptions aren't factual; they show us what we want to see. This sensorial world of physicality is completely ruled by chaos.

The chaos of the physical world exists to serve as natural resistance, which strengthens us. A body builder requires increasing resistance in order to continue to build muscle mass. The chaotic physical world provides the resistance we require to be spiritual body builders. The chaos of the physical dimension (in which we function with our five physical senses) gives us the stimulus we need to turn within, where we find an array of additional spiritual senses and resources to successfully transcend the limits of physicality. The chaos is not here to hurt me; quite to the contrary, it is here to help me build spiritual muscle mass.

The whole idea of Satan can be considered in a new and different way; a way that is empowering rather than disempowering.

I do not discount the activity of the deceptive intelligence, nor do I seek to underestimate or minimize the degree of trickery, mayhem, mischief, and destruction it will seek to involve and engage me in. There is indeed a destructive influence operative upon us that must be countered internally by invoking the amazing grace of God. So while I do not ignore—or deny the existence of—the influence that is fearful of my Godliness, I have chosen to see the Universe as God space, and quite friendly. When the darkness arises within my being, I must choose yet again. I must choose how to cope with the darkness. Do I flee? Do I cower in the corner?

My choice is to pray in each moment the darkness arises. When I remember the powerful words of the beloved son of God, I remember I am the light of the world. The darkness flees from the light. It's not the other way around.

There is never a need to flee the darkness, nor cower in fear. There is only a need to invoke God's amazing grace and allow God, the angels, and the Holy Spirit to work on our behalf, dispelling all darkness. I do nothing of my own accord.

Challenging my disempowering belief and releasing my way of looking at the dark, evil forces, I came to the wonderful discovery of my answer to Einstein's question. Yes, this is indeed a friendly universe. It became, for me, the only loving way to look upon our world.

I recently had an experience that illustrates this point, when I visited Luray Caverns, situated in the mountains of Virginia. The entry point to the caverns begins with a set of stairs that descend into what feels like the bowels of the earth. Each step carried me deeper into the cool dampness of one of Mother Earth's most intriguing caves. As I made my descent, what struck me most—and immediately—was the darkness, the total void of any and all light. The darkness was hauntingly quiet. Tiny lights along the path were the only barrier between us and total black.

I ascertained the shift in energy within myself as I treaded deeper into the caverns and felt the darkness in some spaces envelop me like a thick, black velvet curtain. The tour guide asked our group to stay together and close to her. It was easy for me to comply with that request, considering that my childhood fear of a monster under the bed was beginning to come back to mind. I chuckled at myself and at the thought that a monster could be with us in the cave. Even still, I kept close to the tour guide. *You never know*, I heard one of my inner—and quite irrational— fear voices say in a deep voice.

We finally reached the lowest and deepest part of the caverns, according to our tour guide. I was relieved at her proclamation. The news meant we'd soon be ascending.

It felt strange down there. It was truly another world, like nothing I had seen on Planet Earth before. Being deep in the caverns brought up feelings of fear and excitement simultaneously.

With almost each step, my attention turned to the tiny lights along the path. I marveled at how even the tiniest bit of light could easily dispel the darkness for several feet around it.

I got to thinking about those tiny little lights in Luray Caverns and what they have to do with me. The more I contemplated, the clearer I became about the whole idea of light and dark, and the more joyful I became in my belief that I do indeed live in a friendly universe.

Yes, there is darkness. And yes, it runs from the light. Darkness has no choice but to flee the light. It cannot do otherwise. The light is a force which cannot be stayed, stopped, or denied.

The same is true of God. God is the Light of our lives, the Light that dispels the thickest darkness. Love is the brightest light there is. There is nothing that can stay God's light of love in your world.

God is rapturously in love with you, keeping you guarded from the darkness on all sides (and on the inside) with the bright light of love. Wallow in it today.

This idea of challenging our beliefs and standing in personal truth is liberating and empowering, and leads to full, authentic living, the kind of life God dreams for you, in which you know you are loved fully, supported always, and guided wisely.

The unchallenged belief is the most powerful.

Einstein's question is answered by King David, whose words are quoted at the beginning of this chapter. Here is the scripture passage again, variously stated:

"But now the Lord my God has given me peace on all my borders. I have no enemies, and there is no danger of attack."
1 Kings 5:4 (GNT)

"But now the Lord my God has given me rest on every side, so that there is neither adversary nor evil confronting me."
1 Kings 5:4 (AMP)

"But now the Lord my God has given me peace on every side; I have no enemies, and all is well."
1 Kings 5:4 (NLT)

Thoughts for Today

I am blessed of God and there is nothing to oppose, block, or prevent my good.

All is well.

I am the light of the world.

God's love shines brilliantly in my world, dispelling all darkness and every negative influence.

All is well.

There is nothing to fear.

I am happy and joyful, protected and safe.

I enjoy absolute well-being in mind, body, and spirit.

All is well.

Transition

"For man knows not his time [of death]: as the fishes are taken in an evil net, and as the birds are caught in the snare, so are the sons of men snared in an evil time when [calamity] falls suddenly upon them."
Ecclesiastes 9:12 (AMP)

"Nothing real can be threatened. Nothing unreal exists. Herein lies the peace of God."
A Course in Miracles

The Angel of Death doesn't make appointments. Today, we got the devastating news that my brother-in-law had a heart attack and, shortly thereafter, transitioned out of this life. He was forty-nine years old, and left behind a wife and three children. Devastating.

Only a pillow can handle these tears. Tissues are no good; they're far too weak to handle the job. They fall apart and leave lint on the face. A handkerchief is not much better. These are the kind of tears that well up and fall in streams in the darkness. They hit the pillow and sink in. The pillow can handle it. Some tears can only be handled by a pillow.

I called my mother-in-law to console her and assure her of my prayers and presence. She recounted to me how she had lost her mother and her father. She'd lost all of her brothers and sisters too, she said. And nothing, none of the deaths, prepared her for the feeling she has now, the utter despair, grief, and hopelessness of losing a child. There are no words; the heartache is so wretched, so profound.

It's not like all the other deaths we've experienced before can prepare us for what we feel now. Nothing prepares us.

There is not a moment without tears. Maybe they fall, maybe they don't. Either way, the tears are there. Always right there.

So, we walk about during the day trying to make sense of washing dishes and putting out trash and making beds and food—trying to pretend we can do the activities our day requires, like brushing teeth and washing a face. The mundane becomes monumental.

And all of it is done in a haze of grief, under a canopy of darkness. It's done blindly, eyes are on the task, but there is no seeing of what is being done. There is just the doing of it. That's all. All the while, the eyes are fixed on the face that has left and will never be seen again. The eyes are fixed on the hands and feet that left, the funny walk, the smile. No, the eyes are definitely not on what is being done in the walking-around life.

For several moments, in the conversation with my former mother-in-law, I was speechless. What do I say to a dearly loved woman who has just tragically lost her firstborn son? I didn't know what to say other than "We love you; we are praying for you; he lived a good life, a very good life." Does that suffice? I don't know. What did she want me to say? I don't know. I don't know what I wanted me to say. So I didn't say much. There are no words, really.

There are no words, yet I did what writers do. I wrote. And I prayed:

Dearest Holy God,
I find some little shred of rest and comfort in knowing that death is simply transition. While it seems we were suddenly torn from someone we deeply love, it is not a loss. It is simply a transition. Tony made his transition out of

his body not made with human hands back to Spirit, back to the Source, back home. He let go of his earth suit, that's all. He is still just as alive now as he was before his transition.

I pray for You to enfold us all in the greatest love there is. I know You as the God of all comfort. I pray for all of us who are still here and who shared life with my brother-in-law to be comforted, and to know we are being held and rocked in the arms of God today. I pray for all the tears we've shed—and are still shedding— over our human dear ones who have transitioned back to God.

I pray for us all. Thank you, God, for the healing power of your love. Amen

Thoughts for Today

Death is simply transition; my loved ones who have crossed over are still near and dear to me.

I am resting in the arms of the Divine.

I entrust my grieving heart to God.

Love guides me to healing, wholeness, and happiness.

I am one with divine love, which takes care of all my loved ones who have crossed over.

I trust, accept, and flow with the circle of life.

I am enfolded in the comforting arms of God today, as I fondly remember those I love who no longer abide in this earthly temple not made with human hands.

God's love enfolds them now.

Beauty

"Happy (blessed, fortunate, enviable) is the man who finds skillful and godly Wisdom, and the man who gets understanding [drawing it forth from God's word and life's experiences]."
Proverbs 3:13 (AMP)

"We must first clarify our own vision, then we shall become as lights, lighting the way for others."
Ernest Holmes, *Science of Mind*

I recently heard a definition that was new to me, for the word "understanding." It was defined as "getting under a thing." I hadn't thought of it in that sense and the idea stuck with me. It had the ring of truth. This is true understanding, for what we see on the surface is rarely the truth of the situation. This definition of understanding got me to thinking about all the situations in my life I had labeled as ugly, or wrong, or bad. It got me to thinking about all the events that I'd called tragic, terrible, or horrible. I thought of some of the worst experiences of my life, and I came to see a commonality: underneath all the things I had called ugly, there was sublime beauty.

This fits with my idea and concept of God, which is that God is love and God is in all, through all, omnipotent, omnipresent, and omniscient. I know God is in all, so it only follows that God must be in every situation, even the ones I call ugly, harmful, hateful, or just plain wrong. Even in the worst of the worst, God is there. God is omnipresent, everywhere present at all times.

My eyes have worked against me. They are wonderful tools, yet they are so often fooled. They look at something and though I could almost swear I know what I'm looking at, in reality, I don't know what I'm truly beholding at all. What I perceive through my human eye in any given moment may be wholly inaccurate.

The first time this idea was introduced to me, I rebelled. I remember the day well; it was the first time I picked up a book titled *A Course in Miracles*. One of the early lessons for students studying the Course is to repeat this idea: *Nothing I see means anything*.

My mind refused to take that ride. I had so filled everything in my world with meaning, based upon my limited perceptions of reality, that I just put the book down and dismissed it as foolish.

Though I put the book down, the idea lingered: nothing I see means anything.

Not long after, I was driving in my car while listening to one of my favorite life coaches, Tony Robbins. He was talking about relationships and how we often go wrong in relationships because we give incidents and events meaning.

Most of the time, we give incidents and events an inaccurate meaning. My daughter and I were discussing this concept and I offered her an example.

Say you're going on a date. You've both agreed that your date will meet you at your house at 7:00 P.M. At 7:00 P.M., the date isn't there, and there's no phone call. At 8:00 P.M., your date still isn't there and there's still no phone call. By now, you may be a little heated. You call your date, but no one answers. At 9:00 P.M., your date still isn't there and there's been no communication. At this point, you may be beyond heated. At 9:30 P.M., the phone rings and you get new information. Your date was in an accident and was taken to the hospital. The accident occurred down the street from your home, and it occurred at about 6:45 P.M.

Now how do you feel? Does your whole attitude shift?

If so, your shift in attitude probably has to do with definitions and meanings. With no information one way or the other, we are apt to make up stories about what things mean. If a person is late and they don't call, we have a whole host of things we think it means: this person is insensitive, this person is disorganized and never gets anywhere on schedule, this person gets distracted so easily and is probably somewhere hanging out and completely lost track of time. On and on we can go, giving situations, events, and incidents meaning. Often, the definitions and meanings we make up are skewed to the negative. When I engage in defining events, it's not the most positive use of my mental energies. The definitions and meanings don't usually cast the other person in a good light, either.

My daughter got the point; when we make up what something means, we cause undue stress to ourselves and others involved. Most of the time, the meanings we invent are not the truth of the matter.

I appreciate Tony Robbins's solution, which was to simply ask yourself, "What else could this mean?' This is a powerful question and it directly correlates to what I read in *A Course in Miracles*.

When my eyes look at something, I don't see the full picture. My eyes are useful and valuable, yet they don't see all. My eyes see only the surface, only what is apparently visible. Looking at it from the spiritual perspective, my eyes may only be seeing 1 percent of any given situation. The other 99 percent of any situation only becomes visible to me once I ask, "What does this mean?" If I am certain of what something means, I won't ask any questions. I become closed to new information. I'll rely solely on the limited information my eyes are giving me. When I engage in the practice of relying solely on what my eyes are showing me, I become apt to hurt myself and the people around me.

Understanding comes from asking the question, "What does this mean?" Rather than assuming you know what something means, why not ask? The willingness to ask is a sign of humility. It means acknowledging we may not have all the answers, though we seem to derive a false sense of security when we think we know what's really going on (even when it's clear we don't). It calls for us to let go of little ideas, limited perceptions, and stubborn mental stances to be open to seeing and accepting a broader and more expansive truth.

Look back over the past week. Recall for a moment all the instances where you may have gotten irritated, even if slightly, with someone or something in your world. Now, focus on one particular instance that seems to still cause some upset or dismay within your body when you bring up the memory. Look closely at what unfolded. Did you—in the midst of the flare-up or undesirable event—decide what it all meant? Did you invent definitions? If you did, perhaps you weren't even aware of what you were doing.

Ask yourself, "What else could that have meant?" Or, "What did that situation mean?" Listen carefully for the answer. Now, as you reflect, can you see it somewhat differently? Can you see now, perhaps, that there might have been more to the situation than what you saw?

For me, almost every upset I experience occurs hot on the heels of me defining what's going on, according to my less than true beliefs and inaccurate perceptions. When I have enough presence of mind and heart, I ask, "What does this mean?" The answers are often astonishing.

Become inquisitive. Get curious. Ask what events, incidents, and situations mean. Open yourself to the answers. Never assume you know what you're looking at based upon what your eyes see, which is a practice that keeps you trapped in a human way of looking at the world. When you practice the art of asking questions, you keep yourself open to the spiritual dimension. You transcend humanness. You open yourself to spiritual understanding, to "getting under a thing," and seeing what it really means from a whole new perspective.

Now I ask a lot more questions. There is usually a consistent answer that delivers spiritual understanding: there is sublime beauty under every thing, every event, every person, every happening, and every incident. There is sublime beauty underneath it all.

I have defined and labeled happenings, situations, and people in my life as wrong, bad, ugly, hateful, mean, and/or nasty. One of my all-time, favorite definitions is: "this never should have happened."

The definitions didn't work; they didn't get me where I wanted to be. My definitions and invented meanings inhibited my spiritual understanding, which inhibited my spiritual progress. Are you caught in this trap? Do you think you know what things mean?

Instead, choose to become more present than ever, to watch what the mind does when undesirable conditions arise or when something upsetting has occurred. Ask in prayer what this situation means, rather than assuming.

The other day I was sitting in the nail shop enjoying a pedicure. The television was on. I glanced up and noticed that a crime show was on, the kind that focuses on unsolved crimes and crimes that have been solved, but are now in question because of new DNA evidence that has surfaced. There was a man, who was already incarcerated for another crime, being interviewed from his prison cell. He was being interviewed because he had stated he was responsible for a rape that had been blamed on someone else. The other party was convicted and imprisoned. It seemed he wanted to prove he was the one who committed the rape, so he calmly related the events of the night. He talked about how he chose his victim and what he did. The crime scene matched his recounting of the story.

As I looked at him and listened to his story, something deep within me saw a cry for help, a cry for love. I became aware of what was happening within me at the moment; it was quite different from what I'd so often felt anytime I heard anything about anyone being attacked. Usually, fear, repulsion, disdain, or disgust would arise, often accompanied by terror for my own safety. This day, while sitting there listening to this young man, I felt something new. I asked, what does this mean?

The answer came to me clearly: this is a cry for love. Only hurt people are capable of hurting people. The deeper the hurt within an individual, the greater their capacity to hurt another becomes. This person, this child of God, was deeply hurt. There's only one thing that heals hurt: love. When we hurt, some of us lash out, looking for the love we instinctively crave.

My new way of looking at this young man was profoundly different for me. Rather than immediately despising him, I saw a child who cried for love. Rather than feeling hurt, fearful, or victimized myself, I felt peaceful and calm within. I recommitted myself to knowing love, being love, and sharing love. Love heals all hurts. That is the answer. Underneath it all was a need and a cry for love, a need for this young man to remember himself as a beloved child of God. This is spiritual understanding, getting under a thing. This way of looking at the world is not based upon what human eyes are capable of seeing.

In that holy instant, I was offered a new meaning; a meaning that spontaneously arose from a spiritual perspective of love. This is the heart and essence of understanding.

There is a word of caution here. In the moment we are experiencing a tragedy, or crisis, or pure chaos, we cannot imagine that anything beautiful could result. We don't have understanding when we are in the middle of it. When we are in the fires of life, beauty is neither visible nor do we perceive that it could be anywhere present. When a loved one transitions out of this earthly life, or when illness or disease is present, or when marital or family storms brew, there's no beauty clearly evident. In the midst of the storms of life, no beauty can be found or perceived. We see and feel only hurt and pain. Beauty cannot yet be ascertained.

However, in divine unfolding, with much healing and prayer, and with time spent in the presence of the Lord, spiritual understanding begins to unfold. The beautiful lessons encapsulated in life's most painful and tragic experiences begin to emerge. Beauty begins to show herself.

Before you realize it, beauty teaches you so much that you become a teacher. People who are in the midst of grappling with life's tragedies—the very same tragedies you've already successfully triumphed over—start to find their way to you. As they're drawn, you feel compelled to tell them your stories of triumph. You tell them how God brought you through humanly impossible circumstances. As you speak, they are uplifted and encouraged. Each time you tell your victory story, you, your sister, and your brother rise.

You are blessed with spiritual understanding when you have vision. Vision is different from seeing. Vision is what happens when you don't believe everything your limited human eyes show you. Vision is when you perceive the beauty inherent in every situation, every circumstance, every personal interaction, every trial, every tragedy, and every hurt. No matter what it looks like on the surface, no matter what your human eyes say, underneath all, there is sublime beauty.

God's love for you is so full, so expansive, and so maximal, that He placed sublime beauty underneath your every experience. Ask to see it. Ask for spiritual understanding. Then you'll see the world in a whole new way.

Thoughts for Today

There is sublime beauty underneath each life experience.

I ask and I see the beauty.

I am granted with spiritual understanding now.

God's love places a silvery lining underneath all I would label as tragic.

I am safe and sound in mind and body.

Love carries me through all.

I am thankful for all God brought me through and I encourage and inspire myself and others with every victory story I tell!

Hallelujah!

Eden

"And the Lord God planted a garden toward the
east, in Eden [delight]; and there He put the
man whom He had formed."
Genesis 2:8 (AMP)

"What you think of me is none of my business."
Anonymous

There were two rabbis passing through a small
town where there was a house from which the
most heavenly scent wafted. They were enrap-
tured, caught up in a blissful moment.

"Do you smell that heavenly aroma?" the first
rabbi said to the other.

"Yes, I most certainly do, and it's the most
delightful scent I've ever encountered," said the
second rabbi.

They decided to investigate the source of this
most heavenly scent. They knocked on the door
of the home. The man of the house answered.

"Do tell us, what is the absolutely heavenly scent coming from your home?" inquired the first rabbi.

Not knowing what they were referring to, the man answered with a question, "What scent?"

The second rabbi replied, "The smell that is coming from your home, it's so sweet, it can only be compared with the scent that must have emanated from the Garden of Eden."

The man of the house stood in the doorway, not knowing what to say. He invited the two rabbis in. Happy for the opportunity to investigate and being highly curious about this man and his home, the rabbis readily accepted his offer.

Once inside, the rabbis asked if they could look around. The man consented. They began to walk from room to room to find the source of the wonderful aroma. They followed the scent through the house all the way to the closet in the man's bedroom. The rabbis asked if he would open the closet.

"Certainly," he replied.

When he swung open the closet doors, the scent intensified such that the rabbis knew they had found the source. They looked down and their eyes lit upon a plastic bag in the corner of the closet.

"What's in that bag?" asked one of the rabbis, certain it was the source of the delightful aroma.

When he looked at the bag, the man began to squirm. His whole countenance changed. He was clearly uncomfortable.

"Please don't ask me about that bag. It contains a reminder of the worst day of my life! I don't ever want to open that bag again and I don't even want to talk about it!"

The rabbis were certain this was an outstanding spiritual discovery, considering the aroma wafting from the bag and the man's intense emotional reaction at the sight of it.

"Please, will you tell us about what's in that bag?" the rabbis urged. After much encouragement, the man acquiesced.

"Okay," said the man, though it was clear he was troubled.

He began his story. "One day, a friend of mine came to me to borrow money. He needed the money very badly and was in a desperate state. I had never seen him like that before, so I knew it was quite serious. I gave him all I had and it still wasn't enough. I felt so badly for him. This is a very dear friend, and quite trustworthy, so I told him I would go to some of my friends in town to ask for loans on his behalf. This I did. I went to all my friends in town and asked for loans. They all gave me what they could, though it still wasn't enough. I was feeling very down about the whole situation, so I stopped at the town pub to have a drink and ponder what to do next. As I was sitting there, feeling quite glum and looking just as forlorn as could be, I noticed a rowdy group of businessmen who were sitting near me. They had traveled to our town to conduct business. Now that they had successfully completed their business transactions, they were enjoying drinking themselves into a mild stupor. One of them looked at me and asked why I was looking so down when everyone else in the place was having such a good time. I hesitated to explain my plight to someone who was on the verge of a drunken stupor; however, he kept urging me, so I told him why I looked so glum.

"'I have a dear friend who's in dire straits and my efforts to help him are just not enough. After asking all my other friends for loans on his behalf, I still don't even have half the money he needs.'

"'How much money does your friend need?' the half-drunk asked.

"I told him.

"He said, 'I think we can work out a deal. If you'll do something for me, I can help you with the rest of the money you need for your friend.'

"At first, I didn't believe the half-drunk. The only thing that kept me from dismissing him entirely was his appearance. After all, he looked like he had plenty of money, as did his friends. I was intrigued at the thought of getting the money for my friend, so I told him I was willing to do whatever I had to do. The half-drunk laid out his plan: 'We're having a good time in this town, but what would really top this night off would be some good entertainment. Would you put on this clown suit we have and walk through town wearing it? It'll be such a good time! Is it a deal?'

"I thought his request was quite simple and a little too good of an offer. So I asked for clarity. 'You mean all I have to do is put on this clown suit and walk through town with it on and you'll give me the rest of the money I need for my friend?'

'Yep! That's right' said the half-drunk.

'And he won't have to pay you back?'

'That's right; the money I give you will be payment for your entertainment services.'

"Not wanting to delay, for fear that the half-drunk might rescind his offer, I jumped up and yelled, 'It's a deal!' and enthusiastically shook his hand. I grabbed the clown suit from him and put it on over my clothes. Then I opened the door to the drinking hall and walked out onto the street, certain that this would be the easiest money I ever made. The drunken businessmen were right behind me. By now it was late at night and most of the townspeople were in bed. I prayed no one would recognize me. We began our walk to the end of town. I immediately felt a twinge of embarrassment by all the noise the drunks were making behind me, but I kept walking and hoping no one I knew would see me.

"By the time we'd covered just a short distance, the ruckus was so great that most of the townspeople had awakened. Our little entourage had turned into a parade and I was the fool of the evening, right out in front. The disturbed townspeople began yelling obscenities at us from their windows. Some were so angry they threw trash at me. I can't say that I blame them; from their vantage point, I looked like the ring leader.

"I kept walking, becoming more and more humiliated by the second. The drunks kept up their ruckus behind me, getting louder and more obnoxious than I could've ever imagined. I cursed myself for having agreed to do this. *Is this worth the money? How can I ever show my face in this town again?* It was horrible. It went on like this for over an hour as we made our way to the end of town.

"When we reached the end of town, I was humiliated. My clown suit was covered with stains from the trash that had been angrily hurled at me. The drunks, howling with laughter, had gotten their entertainment. Just as we had agreed, the half-drunk took a wad of money from his pocket and handed me the contracted amount. He and his friends thanked me for a good laugh and for the best time they'd ever had in our small town. Then they all turned and left.

"There I stood, covered in trash, smelling horrible and feeling foolish. I looked at the wad of cash in my hand and knew that my friend would be taken care of. That was the only little ray of light I could find that night. Like I said, it was the worst night of my life.

"That bag has the clown suit in it that I wore that night. I came home, took it off, and stuffed it into that bag. I threw the bag as far back into the closet as I could."

The rabbis looked knowingly at each other and smiled. Then they both gazed lovingly at the man, smiling the whole while. He wondered what was so pleasing to them. There was silence.

After a while, the first rabbi spoke. "You are a blessed child of God. The reason we are smiling is because that night, in your embarrassment and humiliation, your ego was utterly destroyed. Your inner being was not affected by the events of the evening, yet your ego was smashed to pieces in one night. That is why this bag has the heavenly scent emanating from it that it does, for in your act of complete unselfishness, in which you were willing to be humiliated in front of this entire town to help a friend, you gained a place in heaven instantly."

This is one of my favorite stories from the spiritual tradition and path known as Kabbalah (which is based upon the first five books of the Bible).

I think of this story and how it relates to an experience I had when my cell phone was turned off. My bill was sky high and I didn't pay it. The phone company did what phone companies do when they don't get their money on time: they interrupt.

So, there I was with my cell phone turned off. I knew it was going to happen, so it was no surprise. Further, the money was in the bank to pay what they were asking.

This experience was rich in lessons for me. It brought me face-to-face with the remaining shreds of what was once one of my deepest fears: looking bad in the eyes of other people. I had discovered an unsettling trait about myself: I was overly concerned with what people thought of me. I have spent countless hours worrying, or at least wondering, what "they" might think if I did this or that.

What would the neighbors think? Or *what would my parents think?* Or, *what would "they" think?* When questions like these weren't taking center stage in my mind, they were milling around in the background. There was this incessant drive to please outside parties, this need to be approved by them, along with a deeply imbedded fear of being ostracized. I was anxious about other parties and keeping them happy at all costs, even to my denial or detriment. Often, I wasn't even clear about who I was trying to appease at the time. That didn't stop me from trying.

There is, of course, an appropriate level of concern over what we look like to others. This healthy concern causes us to get up in the morning and brush our teeth and comb our hair. This level of healthy concern moves us to buy clothing that is complimentary so as to present ourselves attractively. It's the motivating factor that gets us to look in the mirror and make adjustments before we walk out the door.

This level of care and concern is indeed uplifting and necessary for successful functioning in the world.

What I am referring to as my negative tendency is the driving need to look good in the eyes of other people to such an extent that it would cause me to make decisions that are not self-loving. This condition is a disease of the mind. Only a diseased mind state would cause me to be more concerned about what other people think of me than I would be with what I think of me. Going deeper, it is truly a diseased mind state to be more concerned with what other people think of me than I am with what God knows me to be.

I call this condition a disease because it causes negative outcomes.

When we're overly concerned with how we look to other people, we become inclined to act in ways that keep us from our highest good.

When I get caught up in the internal whirl-wind produced by the "what would people think" line of questioning, I sacrifice my personal truth. I give up what's important to me. I forego responding wholeheartedly to my Inner Voice of Wisdom. I deny my Inner Knowing for what someone else is soliciting me to engage in. Denying who I am to look good to someone else issues from a diseased mind state that precedes and initiates destructive behaviors and negative outcomes.

The good news is, all disease states have cures. This condition can be healed. What's the cure?

God's unconditional love is the healing miracle, which informs and supports self-love, and reminds us of our oneness with all that is.

Any need for external validation is a hole that can only be filled with love. It can be filled with no other thing. All attempts to fill this love-shaped hole with anything other than love will fail and cause pain and suffering in the process. I am reminded of my son, Cory, who, when he was a toddler, would spend what seemed like hours investigating why his round pegs would not fit into square holes. He seemed fascinated by the whole affair; even though his incessant banging never got him the result he was after.

When we seek to gain the affections of someone else by trying to please them, we're vainly attempting to force the peg of external validation into the love-shaped hole within. The two don't fit together. Unconditional love does not, and will not, accommodate or abide the need for external validation. We have a choice. We can choose people-pleasing, to our detriment and frustration, or we can choose to fill ourselves with God's unconditional love, which manifests as abiding self-love and is the path to blissful living. You choose.

When my son was successful at putting the round pegs into the round wooden holes, he'd be delighted. The same is true for us. All intentions and desires to allow God's unconditional love to fill us will lead to peaceful tranquility and delight in mind, heart, and body.

I thought I already knew this. I thought I was cured of my sickness to please people and look good to them. I thought I was completely over that. Apparently not.

So I sat and examined myself for the real reason I was viscerally upset when my cell phone was cut off. The real reason I was agitated is because I perceived the incident to be embarrassing, just like the gentleman who donned the clown suit in the story.

The stream of thoughts I allowed to race through my mind sounded something like this: *What will my friends and family think when they try to call me and my cell phone is off? They'll think I don't have money to pay the bill. I'll look like a trifling idiot. I'll look like I don't have it together. This looks a mess. I'd better do something about it immediately before anyone calls me. I'll go to the bank and take money out and pay the bill right away before anyone knows my cell phone is cut off.*

My mind had become engulfed in its own little self-created tornado. None of the thoughts were productive or self-loving. All the thoughts centered on other people and what they might think of me.

Thank God for the Holy Spirit. Earlier that day, I'd prayed for guidance. I'd spoken an intention to be open to the direction and correction of the Holy Spirit. Thank God—just as I was being swept up in my own fear-inducing mental tirade—the Inner Voice of Wisdom stepped in with a new and refreshing stream of truth and a thought-provoking question or two that arrested and corrected my diseased thinking on the spot.

Inner Voice of Wisdom: "Events only mean what you decide they mean."

I take this as my opportunity to argue my position with the Inner Voice of Wisdom. *I know what this means. This means I must be a trifling idiot. This means I must be irresponsible, which means I must not be good with money and I never will be. This means I don't keep my word and people will never trust me. This means . . .*

I am interrupted in the middle of listing all the meanings I've invented.

Inner Voice of Wisdom: "What is there to learn here?"

What is there to learn here? I don't know and I don't care. I just need to get my cell phone back on this minute! Now, let's see how fast I can get the money out of the bank and get over to the cell phone store to quickly turn my phone back on before anyone notices.

The Inner Voice of Wisdom is silent. I am silent. Then, something happens. Something in my mind opens. Something in my spirit shifts. I feel like I am filled with light. I feel lighter in my seat. There's something new dawning on me, and in me, that I hadn't previously considered. The question "what is there to learn here?" began to burn its way into my psyche.

And then came the answers. In an instant, almost like a flash of lightning.

I was learning not to be overly concerned with what people think of me. This was yet another lesson for me to learn to release being more concerned about the thoughts of others than I am for my own well-being.

For much of my life, I'd been so concerned with what people thought that I'd made choices and decisions that were detrimental to me. I was trying, in a futile attempt, to elicit approval from other people rather than resting peacefully in God's thought of me.

The choices and decisions I've made based on what other people thought impoverished me. Never, not ever, did any choice or decision made with "what will people think of me?" as a basis, contributing factor, or consideration, turn out to be for my good. Never.

Years ago, I heard something I'll never forget. It cut right through to the heart of what I am sharing with you here. What I heard was: "What you think of me is none of my business."

I began to use that line, in little ways, feeling that it would somehow help me overcome my addiction to people-pleasing. I tentatively tried it with tiny things, just to see if it would work. Could this new concept free me from a self-imposed prison? The idea sank deeper into my being. I used it a little more. Good things began to happen.

I worked up enough nerve to try it on bigger things. That's when I noticed a trend: my choices and decisions were becoming more self-loving. I was no longer regularly sabotaging myself for what I thought would make other people happy, all the while failing miserably because I really have no clue what would make someone else happy. It's not my job to make anyone else happy anyway. I have my hands full making myself happy.

My new practice was paying off. As I began to see the positive and profitable fruits of my new and different choices and decisions, I committed myself to developing a new belief: *I am only concerned with what God thinks of me. I will gather my feelings of self-worth from the solid and lov-*

*ing foundation of what God thinks of me. What
other people think of me is no longer going to be
a consideration when making my choices and
decisions.*

I stood up for myself and voted for me. There
is an aspect of my consciousness which knows I
am inherently loved and valued by God. I need
the approval of no one. I came here already fully
approved by God.

There is an aspect of your consciousness that
holds this truth too. You know, within your being,
you are inherently loved and valued by God. You
need no one's approval. You are pre-approved by
God.

I was learning a valuable lesson on the day my
cell phone was turned off: trying to seek the approval of others leads to harm and mayhem.

Conversely, resting in my pre-approved sta-
tus with God leads to peace, joy, harmony, and
prosperity.

Besides, to talk to God, I don't even need a cell
phone.

Back to that question that began to burn a hole
in my psyche: "What is there to learn here?"

I am learning that when I feel embarrassed, I
need to move toward the source of embarrassment rather than away from it. There is healing
in embarrassment. Embarrassment brings me

face-to-face with my fears so I can dispel them for the powerless myths they are. Embarrassment only humiliates and desecrates my ego. My divine, most holy self remains perfectly unaffected by events I would deem embarrassing.

I am learning to make my choices and decisions based upon what's best for me in each moment as I am led, guided, and informed by the Holy Spirit.

I am learning to make choices and decisions that lead to my highest well-being.

I am learning to be an excellent and wise steward over all God entrusts to me.

I am learning to slow down. When I think fast, I seem to hurt myself.

I am learning to let go and let God.

Yes, Holy Spirit, I am learning.

Thoughts for Today

I am fully approved by God.

God's love fills my love-shaped space within.

I draw from it and its sweetness delights me.

I am learning I need only God.

I am free of the need for approval from others.

I am free.

I am free of the need to please other humans.

I am free.

*I make choices for my fullest well-being and
my highest good.*

Gratitude

"O give thanks to Jehovah, you people, for
he is good; For his loving-kindness is to time
indefinite."
Psalms 107:1 (NWT)

"To speak gratitude is courteous and pleasant,
to enact gratitude is generous and noble, but to
live gratitude is to touch Heaven."
Johannes A. Gaertner, *Worldly Virtues*

I am deeply grateful for you. You have shared
part of your life with me by reading these chapters, and I've shared much of myself with you.
We are kindred spirits, you and I, traveling
the spiritual path to higher living through enlightened being.

Gratitude has been the catalyst that has effected
great transformation for me. When I was challenged on all fronts, I followed Oprah's recommendation and the ideas of Sarah Ban Breathn-

ach (author of *Simple Abundance and The Simple Abundance Journal of Gratitude*) and began to keep a gratitude journal. I made that decision in the year 1996. There's so much to say about the power of gratitude, the space here only allows me to get started. Rather than giving you a litany of reasons to be grateful, I decided to share with you selected entries from my Gratitude Journal. It is the fall of 1997.

8/30/1997–Thankful for my mom being here.

9/2/1997–Thankful for Sarai, she's a beautiful girl.

9/2/1997–Thankful for our great weekend in Virginia Beach with Mom and kids.

9/3/1997–Thankful for laughing so much watching Damon Wayans comedy special on HBO late last night—he was a riot!

9/6/1997–Thankful for the good day with my kids—we had fun at the park.

9/8/1997–Thankful for a truly great relationship with my kids—we laugh, talk, laugh, talk—it's great!

9/20/1997–Glad to have C. in my life; she saw another year, thanks to the love of God above. She is a good person.

9/20/1997–Thankful for hanging at J.'s today—we had a great time! T. was entertaining to the utmost! We laughed 'til we cried.

9/20/1997–Thankful my car is still working!

9/21/1997–Thankful for bread to eat another day and that I don't have to food shop constantly, meals for school taken care of—breakfast and lunch. Thank the Lord!

9/21/1997–Thankful for R.'s crazy humor that always brings a smile.

9/22/1997–Thank the Lord! P. called me for an interview! Sounds like a great position to hold me over 'til American Express Financial Advisors.

9/22/1997–Thank the Lord: we were able to rent a car tonight—after my car went up today, transmission.

9/22/1997–Thank the Lord: R. is helping me out with getting car fixed! What a gem!

9/22/1997–Thank the Lord for the Karate lesson for me and Cory—my kids and I had a great time walking to Chatsworth with them—we had great "QT" together. This day started all wrong, but it ended all right!

9/28/1997–Thankful to have a beautiful dinner with my babies!

9/28/1997–Thankful R. said he would give me $2,000 to either fix my car or buy another. He's very special!

9/29/1997–Happy and thankful to the Lord above for helping me get this rental car—I was praying. The Lord is good!

9/29/1997–Thankful I got some exercise at Karate class—I enjoyed it.

9/30/1997–Thankful to D. for giving me R.'s phone number at Apple Ford. I need a car!

9/30/1997–Thankful to R. for giving me name of Eastern Motors—where your job is your credit!!

9/30/1997–Thankful for C.—she's my nearest and dearest friend.

9/30/1997–Thankful for my relationship with L.

9/30/1997–Thankful for my next interview with American Express on Friday, 10/3.

10/3/1997–Thankful that my interview with American Express went well—invited back for next interview on Wednesday, 10/15 at 1 PM!

10/3/1997–Thankful to C. for taking my kids to New York tonight.

10/3/1997–Thankful to Mom for saying okay to let kids come and stay for the weekend.

10/4/1997—My birthday—Sooo thankful—R. came over—took me out to dinner; had a wonderful time at the Inner Harbor. Picked me up from home, bought a bouquet of flowers and a card. The card had a check enclosed for $3,000!!! For a car!!! Yippee! 10/4/1997—My birthday—Thankful to the Lord Jah that I have lived another year.

When I read my own entries, after a dozen years, what strikes me is the sheer simplicity of it all. Most days, I was thankful for the often overlooked blessings, like taking a walk with my kids or watching a television show I found hilarious. Each day, because I was intentionally looking for things to be grateful for, I noticed all the little things I'd probably overlooked for years. With my new gratitude outlook, my entire world began to offer me reason after reason to be joyously grateful.

We don't have to wait for the big things in life to be grateful. Each day, there is much to be thankful for: a smile from a stranger, a door held for an extra few seconds, a nod from a mate who's listening intently, a really good passage from a book, an amazing cup of coffee, a stunning sunrise, a sunset in colorful splendor, a giggle from the baby, a purr from the cat, a lick from the puppy. All of these are reasons to be immensely grateful.

Turn on the gratitude when you're experiencing trouble. In reading my journal, I am reminded of Bessie, my fifteen-year-old Toyota Cressida, who was on her way to the car graveyard. She tried to hang in there, but her transmission just couldn't make it. We had to let her go. I spoke gratitude for her each time she worked well for me and my kids and I spoke gratitude when she died. I was happy for the rental car and happy that the wonderful man I was dating at the time (who later became my husband) gave me a gift of $3,000 for a car. I took the money and went to an auction where I found a beautiful, garage-kept car. I paid cash for it and drove it for the next couple of years. My kids and I traveled in comfort, style, and safety. It was truly a gift. A happy and grateful frame of mind attracts the full support of the Universe.

In the times we're experiencing difficulty, it's especially important to turn on the gratitude and keep it flowing. When you consistently and happily speak thankfulness over everything in your world, you set up a current of positive universal energy that will supply your every need. Your loving and ecstatic gratitude is your greatest magnet for good.

God's unconditional love supports you forever. Be grateful for all you are, for all you have and for all you are able to do. You are a gift and a divine blessing.

I am so grateful for you and for what God is now doing in your life. May you be richly blessed beyond all human comprehension and may everything you touch succeed.

With infinite and eternal gratitude,
Valerie Love

Thoughts for Today

I am joyously grateful!

*Everything in my world is cause for thankful-
ness—if I like it, great!*

If I don't, great!

The things I don't like only make me stronger.

*I make it a practice to take inventory of the
multitude of blessings that are deposited by
Spirit onto my doorstep each day.*

I lie in bed considering how blessed I am.

I fall asleep with a smile on my face.

*I give thanks for my dearly-loved friends, fam-
ily, and intimate partner, and I express my
gratitude for their loving presence.*

I am aware. I am joyful. I am deeply grateful.

Amen.

Bibliography

Bible Translations Used in This Text:

Amplified Bible (AMP). Grand Rapids, MI: Zondervan Publishing, 2001.

Good News Bible—TEV (GNT). New York, NY: American Bible Society, 2001.

Life Application Study Bible: New Living Translation-2 (NLT). Carol Stream, IL: Tyndale House Publishers, 2004.

New World Translation of the Holy Scriptures (NWT). Brooklyn, NY: Watchtower Bible and Tract Society, 1984.

Books Cited:

Allen, James. *The Wisdom of James Allen*. San Diego, CA: Laurel Creek Press, 1997.

Berg, Michael. *Becoming Like God: Kabbalah and Our Ultimate Destiny*. New York, NY: Kabbalah Publishing, 2004.

Breathnach, Sarah Ban. *Simple Abundance: A Daybook of Comfort and Joy*. New York, NY: Grand Central Publishing, 1995.

Butterworth, Eric. *The Universe is Calling: Opening to the Divine Through Prayer*. New York, NY: Harper Collins, 1994.

DeStefano, Anthony. *A Travel Guide to Heaven*. New York, NY: Doubleday, 2005.

Ferrini, Paul. *Love Without Conditions: Reflections of the Christ Mind*. Greenfield, MA: Heartways Press, 1994.

Gaertner, Johannes A. *Worldly Virtues: A Catalogue of Reflections*. Grand Rapids, MI: Phanes Press, 2002.

Gee, Margaret. *Words of Wisdom: Quotes by His Holiness the Dalai Lama*. Kansas City, MO: Andrews McMeel Publishing, 2001.

Holmes, Ernest: *Science of Mind: A Philosophy, A Faith, A Way of Life*. New York, NY: Tarcher Putnam, 1998.

Kinnear, Willis. *30-Day Mental Diet: The Way to a Better Life*. Lakewood, CA: Science of Mind Publications, 1963.

Lazaris. *Lazaris: The Sacred Journey - You and Your Higher Self*. Beverly Hills, CA: Synergy Publishing, Inc. 1987.

Weseman, Tim. *God's Direction is Always Best!* Fenton, MO: CTA, Inc., 2004.

Myss, Caroline. *Anatomy of the Spirit: The Seven Stages of Power and Healing*. New York, NY: Three Rivers Press, 1997.

Ponder, Catherine. *The Dynamic Laws of Prosperity*. Camarillo, CA: DeVorss & Company, 2004.

Price, John Randolph. *Practical Spirituality*. Carlsbad, CA: Hay House, Inc., 1996.

Ruiz, Don Miguel. *The Mastery of Love: A Practical Guide to the Art of Relationship* (Toltec Wisdom Book). San Rafael, CA: Amber-Allen Publishing, Inc., 1999.

Schucman, Dr. Helen. *A Course in Miracles*. Mill Valley, CA: Foundation for Inner Peace, 1976.

Society for the Promotion of Buddhism. *The Teaching of Buddha*. Tokyo, Japan: Society for the Promotion of Buddhism, 1966.

Tolle, Eckhart. *The Power of Now: A Guide to Spiritual Enlightenment*. Novato, CA: New World Library, 1999.

Virtue, Doreen. *Healing with the Angels: How the Angels Can Assist You in Every Area of Your Life*. Carlsbad, CA: Hay House, Inc., 1999.

Williamson, Marianne. "The Meaning of Midlife," *Pure Inspiration,* Issue 8—Summer 2008. Stanhope, NJ: Light-stream Publishing.

Yogananda, Paramahansa. *Scientific Healing Affirmations: Theory and Practice of Concentration*. Los Angeles, CA: Self-Realization Fellowship, 2007.

About the Author

After seven years in the financial services industry as a financial advisor with American Express Financial Advisors, Valerie Love sold her financial planning practice to follow her passions: writing and being an inspirational speaker.

Shortly thereafter, she completed her first book *God Speaks to Me—Stories of Triumph Over Tragedy from Women Who Listened to God* published by Urban Christian Books in November 2007.

After her momentous and life-changing decision, Valerie has never looked back. She is an inspirational speaker and life coach who passionately teaches the art and science of living at full potential.

The author is also President and founder of Live Your Destiny, a self-development company which specializes in personal transformation by offering training, coaching, workshops and retreats which teach and inspire participants to live at full potential with excellence, passion, purpose and power.

Web site:
www.LiveYourDestinyToday.com

The author's e-mail:
valerielove@LiveYourDestinyToday.com

UC HIS GLORY BOOK CLUB!

www.uchisglorybookclub.net

UC His Glory Book Club is the spirit-inspired brainchild of Joylynn Jossel, Author and Acquisitions Editor of Urban Christian, and Kendra Norman-Bellamy, Author for Urban Christian. This is an online book club that hosts authors of Urban Christian. We welcome as members all men and women who have a passion for reading Christian-based fiction.

UC His Glory Book Club pledges our commitment to provide support, positive feedback, encouragement, and a forum whereby members can openly discuss and review the literary works of Urban Christian authors.

There is no membership fee associated with UC His Glory Book Club; however, we do ask that you support the authors through purchasing, encouraging, providing book reviews, and of course, your prayers. We also ask that you respect our beliefs and follow the guidelines of the book club. We hope to receive your valuable input, opinions, and reviews that build up, rather than tear down our authors.

WHAT WE BELIEVE:

—We believe that Jesus is the Christ, Son of the Living God.

—We believe the Bible is the true, living Word of God.

—We believe all Urban Christian authors should use their God-given writing abilities to honor God and share the message of the written word God has given to each of them uniquely.

—We believe in supporting Urban Christian authors in their literary endeavors by reading, purchasing and sharing their titles with our on-line community.

—We believe that in everything we do in our literary arena should be done in a manner that will lead to God being glorified and honored.

—We look forward to the online fellowship with you. Please visit us often at: *www.uchisglorybookclub.net.*

Many Blessing to You!
Shelia E. Lipsey,
President, UC His Glory Book Club